BATTLES IN FOCUS

VICKSBURG

One of the Union
attempts to storm
Vicksburg. On 25 June
a mine containing
2,200 pounds of
gunpowder was
exploded at the 3rd
Louisiana Redan, and
the 45th Illinois
Infantry surged into
the crater. The
Confederates however,
had built a wall behind
the redan and the
attack failed.

BATTLES IN FOCUS

VICKSBURG

T. A. HEATHCOTE

BRASSEY'S

To the Southern gentlemen of VP 62 "The Broad Arrows" Squadron, United States Navy Reserve, with whom the author had the privilege of flying at Jacksonville, Florida.

First published in 2004 by Brassey's

An imprint of Chrysalis Books Group plc

Brassey's
The Chrysalis Building, Bramley Road,
London W10 6SP
www.chrysalisbooks.co.uk

Distributed in North America by:
Casemate Publishing, 2114 Darby Road,
Havertown, PA 19083, USA

T. A. Heathcote has asserted his moral right to be identified as the author of this work.

Library of Congress Cataloging in Publication Data available

British Library Cataloguing-in-Publication Data: a catalogue record for this book is available from the British Library

ISBN 1 85753 339 9

Photographs: PageantPix

Edited and designed by DAG Publications Ltd
Designed by David Gibbons
Edited by Michael Boxall
Cartography by Anthony A. Evans

Printed in Singapore

Introduction, 6

1 THE THEATRE OF WAR, 8
Vicksburg and the Mississippi
The City and the People, 11

2 ARMIES AND LEADERS, 15
The Presidents, 15
Union Generals, 16
Confederate Generals, 21
The Union Naval and Marine Officers, 24
The Confederate Naval Officers, 27
The Armies, 28
Uniforms and Weapons, 33

3 RIVER WARFARE, 34
The River Roads to Vicksburg
The Descent to New Madrid: March – April 1862, 34
The Ascent from New Orleans: April – May 1862, 38
The battles of Fort Pillow and Memphis: May – June 1862, 40
The Naval Attack: June – July 1862, 41
The Arkansas: June – August 1862, 43
Grant's Operations in Northern Mississippi: December 1862 – January 1863, 46

CONTENTS

Sherman's Attack on the Chickasaw Bluffs (The Walnut Hills): December 1862, 48

The Capture of Fort Hindman (The Arkansas Post): January 1863, 51

4 SWAMP WARFARE, 53

The Moves to Outflank Vicksburg, January – April 1863

The De Soto Canal: January – March 1863, 53

The Lake Providence Waterway: January – February 1863, 54

The Queen of the West and the Indianola: February 1863, 56

The Yazoo Pass: February – March 1863, 58

The Deer Creek Expedition: March 1863, 61

The Battle of Port Hudson: March 1863, 65

The March down the River: April 1863, 68

5 LAND WARFARE, 72

The Approach to Vicksburg, April – May 1863

Grierson's Raid: 17 April – 2 May 1863, 72

The Passage of the Mississippi: April 1863, 76

The Battle of Port Gibson: 1 May 1863, 80

The Fall of Grand Gulf: 2 May 1863, 81

The Battle of Champion Hill (Baker's Creek): 16 May 1863, 84

The Battle of the Big Black: 17 May 1863, 90

6 SIEGE WARFARE, 96

The Siege of Vicksburg, 19 May – 4 July 1863

The Defences, 96

First Assault: 19 May 1863, 99

The Second Assault: 22 May 1863, 100

The Siege Campaign, 104

The Cincinnati: May 1863, 106

Continued Resistance, 107

The Continued Approach, 111

The Third Assault: 25 June 1863, 114

The Final Weeks, 115

The Capitulation, 117

The Entry into Vicksburg: 4 July 1863, 120

7 CONCLUSION, 122

Select Bibliography, 124

The Battlefield Today: Tours and Museums, 126

Index, 128

INTRODUCTION

The American Civil War played so momentous a part in the birth of a nation that it has never ceased to fascinate not only the citizens of that country but those of many others whose interests and histories are linked with it. It has been calculated that at least 70,000 books have been published on the subject, together with countless articles, monographs, novels and feature films, all drawing on the dramatic events of the time. This book is designed to provide a narrative of a campaign that may be less well-known than the long duel between the Armies of the Potomac and Northern Virginia, but had its own distinctive features and importance nevertheless. In the words of the former Mississippi pilot Samuel Clemens (who took his pen-name, Mark Twain, from the cry of the steam-boats' leadsmen): 'The war history of Vicksburg had more about it to interest the general reader than that of any other river town. It was full of variety, full of interest, full of the picturesque. Vicksburg held out longer than any other important river town and saw warfare in all its stages, both land and water.'

This book is intended for British as well as American readers, and where relevant I have used terminology which reflects this aim. River vessels, no matter how large, are called boats by British and American sailors alike. Ships are sea-going vessels. Groups of boats are flotillas. Groups of major warships are squadrons. Place-names sometimes differ between Northern and Southern usage, and also between contemporary and modern forms. I have used those given in the Official Atlas of the Civil War published by the United States Government in 1891–95. At the time of the war, African-Americans were generally known by both sides as Negroes, though the term Coloured was recognised as a more polite term. Both expressions are now considered out-moded and, at the risk of seeming anachronistic, I have used the term African-American as one that is both accurate and generally acceptable. Even the name of the war requires consideration. Was it the War of the Rebellion, the War for the Southern Confederacy, the War between the States, or simply the Civil War? To avoid the appearance of partiality, I have used only the last two forms. Finally, although the correct title of the Federal, or national, forces was 'United States' Army or Navy, I have generally followed the convention of calling them 'Union' forces.

I take this opportunity of expressing my gratitude to all those from whose aid and advice I have benefited in the writing of this book, and especially to Matthew Midlane, Director of Studies at the Royal Military Academy Sandhurst; Andrew Orgill, John Pearce and Ken Franklin, of the RMAS Central Library; Ann Ferguson, RMAS Media Resources Library; Gary Sheffield, Defence Studies Department, Joint Services Command and Staff College, Shrivenham; Paul Harris, Department of War Studies, RMAS; Ian Williamson, late of the College of Petroleum Studies, Oxford; Jean Carter, Principal of Enfield College; Paul

Kendall, late of the University of London Royal Naval Unit, and Surgeon Lieutenant-Commander Dennis Freshwater, Royal Navy. I must also pay tribute to my wife for her constant encouragement and support, reading and proof-reading my drafts, and agreeing to accompany me around the watery battle-sites of the lower Mississippi.

In conclusion, I express my admiration for all those American soldiers and sailors who fought in the Vicksburg campaign, and my regard for those of their modern successors with whom I became friends while in NATO Maritime Intelligence. Regardless of national differences, the words of the officially neutral Captain Josiah Tattnall, USN (later Commodore, CSN), when sending a steamer to help the hard-pressed Royal Navy in the battle of the Taku Forts in 1859, seem to me still true: 'Blood is thicker than water'.

T. A. Heathcote
Camberley, June 2003

Union works of Logan's division before the honey-combed redan on the Jackson Road manned by the 3rd Louisiana Infantry.

1
THE THEATRE OF WAR
VICKSBURG AND THE MISSISSIPPI

The mighty River Mississippi, 'The Father of Waters' in the tongue of the Native Americans who lived along its banks, 'Old Man River' to the other peoples who later worked there, flows for more than 2,530 miles from its source in northern Minnesota to the Gulf of Mexico. With its greatest tributary, the Missouri, its length extends over 3,740 miles, draining the second largest catchment area in the world, consisting of all the land between the Rocky Mountains in the west and the Alleghenies in the east and amounting to an area of 1,244,000 square miles. In terms of volume, it is the world's fifth largest river, discharging an average of 612,000 cubic feet of water per second when it finally reaches the sea. Six hundred miles from the sea, its bed is already less than five hundred feet above sea level and, as the gradient decreases, the river flows more slowly and deposits some of the material suspended in its waters to form constantly-shifting shallows, snags and sand-bars. Its course starts to meander through a flood plain built up from this material and forms numerous winding side streams, known as bayous, alongside its main channel. As the current flows faster on the outside of bends and slower on the inside, it makes the outside deeper and the inside shallower, so that over time the meanders become hair-pin shaped. Eventually, the force of the stream cuts through the neck of the peninsula thus created, and finds a new, straighter, course, leaving the original one as an elongated swampy lagoon or 'oxbow'.

The entire Mississippi system extends to 15,000 miles of navigable waterway and became a natural avenue of exploration, development and trade for European colonists and their American successors. As early as 1519, Spanish explorers had mapped the coast of the Gulf of Mexico and discovered the mouth of the Mississippi, which they named the Rio del Espiritu Sancto. In 1541 Hernando De Soto, undertaking the conquest of Florida and its hinterland, came upon the river just below its confluence with the Yazoo. At this point, in one of its great meanders, the Mississippi runs north-east for about five miles, before turning south-west in a hair-pin bend to create a peninsula on its western side. On the opposite bank the land rises steeply in a series of bluffs or cliffs, two to three hundred feet high, composed of the yellowish-red alluvial loam (loess) characteristic of this region and eroded into steep gullies by the heavy winter and spring rains. There, De Soto built Fort Nogales, so-called from the Spanish word for the walnut trees that freely grew there and that gave their name, when the Americans later surveyed the area, to the Walnut Hills on which they stood. Less poetically, the riverside cliffs were known as the Chickasaw Bluffs, and the neck of land across the Mississippi became the De Soto Peninsula.

It was, however, the French explorer La Salle who in 1682 was the first European to descend the river, in the vain hope of reaching the Pacific. He named the vast region between the Great Lakes and the sea 'Louisiana' in honour of his king, but in 1763 France ceded to Spain all her claims to Louisiana west of the Mississippi, and to the United Kingdom all those east of it. In 1803 Bonaparte obliged the Spanish to return their share of Louisiana to France, only to sell it to the infant United States of America, which thereby doubled in size. In 1812 the southernmost part of this territory was admitted to the Union as the state of Louisiana. In 1783 the British claim to West Florida (the area east of the Mississippi and south of Fort Nogales) was inherited by the newly independent United States of America, which seized control of the disputed territory from Spain during the War of 1812. With the spread of American settlement, these territories were admitted to the Union as the States of Mississippi and Alabama in 1817 and 1819 respectively.

Throughout all these changes, the Mississippi grew in economic importance. The difficulty of moving any kind of loads by wagon or pack animal and the physical difficulty of the roads through the Allegheny mountains meant that as frontier settlements moved west they came to rely on water transport to take their produce out and import manufactured items. Some could use the Great Lakes, but most preferred to avoid the costs of this route and used the great river system instead. By the middle of the 18th century, the most economic way of shipping heavy goods between Pittsburg, Pennsylvania, and New York was to send them down the Ohio River and the Mississippi to the port of New Orleans at the river's mouth and from there along the Atlantic coast.

The major problem on this route was the technical one of propulsion. Going downstream, goods could be carried with the current in flat-boats or 'arks', wooden rafts with shacks to shelter the crew. On arriving at their destination, the arks were dismantled and sold for lumber, while the boatmen travelled back overland along the Natchez Trace (the French word for 'trail'). Going up-stream, goods were carried in keel-boats, usually propelled by teams of men with punt-poles. Running-boards allowed the teams to march steadily along the length of the boat, each man in turn resuming his original place so as to keep up a continual momentum. These boatmen, such as Mike Fink, a famous figure in the legends of the West, were a tough and extrovert group and played a significant part in establishing the culture of their place and time. The limits of human muscle-power, however, affected even such men as these, and it took three months to pole a loaded boat upstream from New Orleans to Cincinnati, Ohio. The construction of canals to the Great Lakes in the 1830s and 1840s made the northern route more attractive and did much to bind the Mid-Western states of Ohio, Indiana and Illinois to New York and the North rather than New Orleans and the South. The opening of the Chicago canal in 1848 created a direct link between the Great Lakes and the Mississippi, giving a greater choice of markets and lowering of freight rates.

By this time, two major developments had affected the Mississippi. The first was the invention of the steam-engine and its application to river-traffic. In 1814, the paddle-steamer *New Orleans* made the first run to that city from Pittsburg, Pennsylvania. The steam-boat captains inherited all the spirit of their keel-boat predecessors and became a byword for their refusal to comply with anyone's wishes but their own, or to give way to other vessels of any description. The hazardous tendency of early steam engines to explode when run at high pressure was increased by an even more hazardous one of captains lashing down the safety valves to increase speed. The number of steam tug-boats and transports rose rapidly and by 1846 New Orleans was the fourth busiest port in the world, reflecting the development of its hinterland, encouraged by the ease of steam-boat transportation. As well as their freight holds, the larger steamers had luxurious passenger decks, where travellers whiled away the journeys at the gaming tables, in bars or ballrooms, or similar entertainments. Minstrels and bands were supplemented by a new invention, the Calliope, or musical steam whistle. A big paddle-steamer could be expected to make more than 12 knots, with the most famous upstream run being that of the 'good ship *Robert E. Lee*' which in 1870 covered the 1,228 miles from New Orleans to St Louis, Missouri, in three days, eighteen hours and fourteen minutes, being refuelled from tenders while under way.

The main function of the river-boats, however, was to carry away the cotton that only they were able to move in economic bulk. When railways were built in the South, they mostly served to connect up and supplement existing waterways. In the North, by 1850, railways had succeeded waterways as the main means of transport, and ran east and west, along the country's future axis of development, rather than north and south. Although the South began building railways westwards from its Atlantic ports in the late 1840s, the capital that would have been needed to produce a system as extensive as that in the North was invested in cotton plantations and the slaves to operate them.

By the end of the 18th century, the Industrial Revolution in Europe had produced a technology that could spin and weave cotton in the quantities that would support a mass market. What had previously been a luxury item became readily available to

The levee at Vicksburg, shown here in February 1864. The capture of the city cut the Confederacy in two and opened the course of the great river to navigation by Union vessels.

an expanding population and created a demand for raw cotton that nowhere was so well placed to supply as were the newly acquired southern regions of the United States. New Orleans had been New France's most prosperous commercial centre, and its hinterland had become the home of 'Cajuns', who left the French colony of Acadia when this became the British colony of Nova Scotia in 1713. Nevertheless, the climate, so different from those of France and Spain, deterred settlers from either of these countries, and the Americans, moving westwards, found a land that was, by their standards, largely undeveloped and uncultivated.

The local climate, with its humidity and Fahrenheit temperature both rising to the nineties during the summer, was ideal for the cotton plant. It was also one that could be tolerated by the African-American slaves who had long been used as labour on tobacco and sugar plantations. The plantation system gained a new lease of life in the rich soil of Mississippi and Alabama and, by 1860, 60 per cent of the world's entire cotton supply came from the southern USA. Alongside the plantations were farmsteads producing food for men and animals, dairy cattle, pigs (or 'hogs' as they are still called locally) and pastures for the horses and mules on which inland transport depended. Between them grew up new towns with all the services needed to support the surrounding countryside. The very appearance of the rivers began to change as gangs of slave labour enlarged and connected the natural embankments or levees, to help drain the land, reduce flooding and provide landings for the river-boats.

THE CITY AND THE PEOPLE

One of the towns that grew up on the developing steam-boat and cotton trade was established at the confluence of the Mississippi and the Yazoo, where Fort Nogales had been abandoned by the Spanish in 1803. In 1825, with a population of 150, it received its charter as Vicksburg, after the Reverend Ewet Vick, an unordained Methodist preacher who, with his numerous family and dependants, had developed a settlement there some ten years previously. By 1860, when its first City Directory was published, it had a population of 1,500 and was the second largest municipality in the State of Mississippi. The county seat of Warren County, it could boast a fine court-house, five churches, several schools and academies (including a seminary and convent of the Roman Catholic Sisters of Mercy), two hospitals, three newspapers, hotels, banks, lawyers, land dealers, cotton and slave brokers, and members of all the professions and businesses to be expected in a growing river port. It had a playhouse, a Masonic Hall and even a gas-works, the only one in the State, to provide lighting for streets, homes and places of business. By 1860 Vicksburg was also on one of the South's few railways. The Mississippi Southern Railroad ran for some forty miles eastwards from Vicksburg to Jackson, the State capital of Mississippi, and thence to connections with New Orleans, Tennessee, Alabama and South Carolina. With no bridge across the Mississippi, reliance was placed on ferries to take passengers and freight the half-mile across the river to the Vicksburg, Shreveport and Texas Railroad, running from the De Soto Peninsula to Monroe, Louisiana.

While the respectable inhabitants had their spacious homes and public build-ings high on the bluffs, whence the city's main roads ran in a grid plan down to the river, the less respectable ones provided establishments on the riverside for the traffic on which Vicksburg's prosperity was based. These included various disorderly houses and gambling dens (periodically raided by local guardians of public morals) as well as wharves for the coal on which the boats depended, pens for slaves and animals and warehouses for goods of all kinds, especially the cotton from surrounding plantations. While the upper city sparkled on its sunlit hills, the lower slopes were frequently shrouded in a smog of steam and coal-smoke from the numerous river-boats, combined with mist from the water-side and neighbouring swamps. After the land in the city's eastern hinterland was developed, new plantations were opened to the west, across the Mississippi in Madison, Louisiana, and to the north, in the country between the Yazoo and the Mississippi. There, the swampy and low-lying terrain made settlement more dif-ficult and in 1860 much of it remained an overgrown wilderness of trees and vines, intersected by numerous watercourses.

The new American settlers of the lower Mississippi brought with them the dis-tinctive culture of the Southern States from which they came. They were, to a far greater extent than their Northern neighbours, an ethnically homogeneous peo-ple, drawn mostly from English, Scottish or Northern Irish stock. Generations of frontier life had produced a spirit of independence in both political and person-al life, but their homogeneity led to a conservatism of outlook and a determina-tion to protect their rights and society. In particular, there was a readiness to resort to bloodshed to settle differences. Gentlemen were expected to demand satisfaction for any insult by means of a duel, a custom regarded in the North as no better than bullying and murder. Their example was frequently followed, without the niceties of any code of honour, by yeomen in remote country farms, gamblers in the river-boats and adventurers on the Western frontier.

The upper echelons of society followed the ways of the English landed gentry in which they were rooted, living in the same kind of gracious country houses, surrounded by the same kind of furniture and family portraits, sending their sons to the same kind of universities, dressing their wives and daughters in the same fashions and fabrics, following the same martial traditions and displaying the same nerve at the gaming-table or in the saddle. Indeed, the famous 'Rebel Yell' of the Southern troops, when war between the States came about, was said by some to have originated in the English hunting-field.

To outsiders, the most distinctive feature of that society was bond slavery. Of the twelve million inhabitants of those States that seceded from the Union in 1861, four million were African-Americans, most of them slaves. Indeed, the increase in the number of cotton plantations produced an increase in the slave population. Yet not all Southerners were, or wished to be, slave-owners. Three out of every four had no direct interest in this 'peculiar institution'. At the beginning of the Civil War only 384,000 Americans owned slaves and only 180,000 owned more than ten. Yet the slavery of African-Americans seemed so natural in the South that the word 'slave' was scarcely used. Domestic slaves were generally referred to as 'servants' and plantation slaves as 'hands'. White employees, by contrast, were 'hired help'. To the defenders of slavery, the owners were Christian ladies and gentlemen, humane, generous, and careful of their property if only out of self-interest, while the slaves benefited from their masters' care and were proud to belong to them. At the same time, the slaves were essential for the hard physical work to which, in the local climate, white men were unsuited.

From a more practical standpoint, the claims of abolitionists that (quite apart from any moral or ethical considerations) well-motivated free labour was more efficient than slave labour, had been disproved by the abolition of slavery in the British colonies. Not only had the British Treasury groaned under the cost of compensating the owners, but most former slaves preferred cultivating their own plots to remaining on the plantations as paid employees. Undercut by places where slavery remained in force, the once prosperous planters of the British West Indies had been driven into virtual bankruptcy.

The development of the lower Mississippi gave the South a greater rate of population increase during this period than any other part of the Union. With it came political power in the Federal government, which enacted a series of measures to preserve the institution of slavery on which the Southern economy depended. Most North Americans of the time, like most Europeans, took it for granted that Africans were naturally inferior to themselves, a view that would continue to be widely held on both sides of the Atlantic at least until the middle of the following century. Although public opinion in the northern USA deplored slavery, it was therefore, despite an increasingly influential abolitionist movement, prepared to tolerate it in the South where historically it had existed. Nevertheless, the extension of slavery in States newly admitted to the Union, and the passage into Federal law of measures such as the Fugitive Slave Law (obliging Northern policemen and marshals to act as slave-catchers) caused much resentment. It seemed that it would be only a matter of time before the larger Northern population (by 1860, twenty million against the South's nine million free people) used its majority in Congress to repeal the offending laws and eventually slavery itself would cease to be protected.

Following the United States' Presidential election of 1860 Abraham Lincoln, the Republican candidate, came into office with the overwhelming support of the Northern states. In his inaugural address on 4 March 1861 he stated that he would not interfere with the institution of slavery, but his election was regarded throughout the South (where he had not gained a single vote in the electoral colleges) as a sign that abolition would inevitably follow. Between December 1860 and May 1861 the seven southernmost States of the USA declared their secession from the Union, on the principle that they had the right to leave a federal body which they had freely entered. Together, they formed what was intended to be a new nation, the Confederate States of America, headed by their own President, Jefferson Davis.

On 12 April 1861 Confederate batteries under Brigadier General Pierre Gustave Beauregard, lately Superintendent of the United States Military Academy, West Point, fired on the Federal garrison of Fort Sumter, Charleston, South Carolina. Lincoln had not been disposed to force war over the issue of slavery, though he had earlier declared (in a phrase borrowed from the Gospels) that a house divided against itself could not stand and therefore it must inevitably become all slave or all free. His prime concern was the preservation of the Union and his inaugural address had stressed his determination to resist the claim that any State had the right to secede from it. As for the slaves, he had declared that if he could preserve the Union only by freeing them all, or only by keeping them all in bondage, he would do either of those things, and if he could preserve the Union only by freeing some and keeping the rest in bondage, he would do that too. Now that the war had started, and with only a small regular army at his disposal (mostly deployed on the western frontiers or in coastal garrisons), he called on all the States of the Union to raise volunteers for the suppression of rebellion and the defence of Federal author-ity. The North responded to his call. Convinced that their quarrel was right and honourable, men flocked to join the newly raised Volunteer regiments and demanded to be led south to fight the 'Johnny Rebs'.

Southerners were equally sure of the justice of their own cause. Between April and June 1861 Virginia, Arkansas, North Carolina and Tennessee seceded from the Union and became the northern tier of the Confederacy, extending its territory up the lower Mississippi to include two of the river's great tributaries, the Cumberland and the Tennessee. With their martial traditions and proud independent spirits (which in the long run actually proved less well-suited to the changed nature of war-fare than those of an industrialised Northern society), the people of the South were confident of their ability to defeat the Yankee rabble and defy Lincoln's tyranny.

The Mississippi State Convention to decide the issue of secession was held on 7 January 1861. Vicksburg, whose livelihood depended on free navigation of the great river system, was one of only two constituencies whose delegates were mandated to vote for the status quo. But when the Ordinance of Secession was carried, and Mississippi became, after South Carolina, the first state to leave the Union, the great majority of Vicksburg's inhabitants rallied to the Secessionist cause. The city's two existing militia companies (the Sharpshooters and the Southrons), patriotic citizens who had voluntarily undertaken military training in their spare time, were joined by four new locally raised corps, the Warren Dragoons, the Vicksburg Light Artillery, the Warren County Guards, and the Hill City Cadets. Three companies of infantry and four guns from the artillery were deployed north of their city, on the bluffs where Fort Nogales had once stood. From there, on 11 January 1861, three months before Fort Sumter was fired upon, Vicksburg's gunners fired their first shots of the war, against the United States' flag on the peaceful steamboat *O. A. Tyler*, bringing a cargo of merchandise from far-off Cincinnati.

ARMIES AND LEADERS

THE PRESIDENTS

Abraham Lincoln

By virtue of his office, the President of the United States of America is also Commander-in-Chief of the nation's armed forces. Some Presidents, beginning with George Washington, have been successful generals and several others can claim to have served as soldiers, if only for a short period. Among the latter was Abraham Lincoln, the sixteenth President, elected in 1860. Born in 1809 in a log cabin in Kentucky, he grew up with his family in the backwoods of south-western Indiana and in 1830 moved on with them to Illinois, where he worked in a variety of humble occupations including, famously, that of rail-splitter, turning timber into the posts and rails used for agricultural fences. He also found employment on the western rivers and went down the Mississippi on a flat-boat, which gave him an understanding of the importance of this part of the country that never left him. With little formal education, he studied grammar and law and began to think of taking up politics. After a brief period of military service during the Black Hawk War of 1832, when the Sauk and Fox Indians were terrorising western Illinois, Lincoln entered the Illinois legislature and began to practise as a lawyer. He emerged as a powerful debater, with a gift for language couched in the phrases of the King James Bible, for clear logical argument and for illustrating his case with home-spun story-telling. He was defeated in his bid to become senator for Illinois in 1856, but his views on the slavery question and his skill as an orator brought him to national prominence. In May 1860 he was nominated Republican candidate for the presidency of the United States and was elected in the following December. When war with the Confederacy began, he left operational decisions to his generals, encouraging those who succeeded, but removing those who failed the test of battle and replacing them with those who seemed likely to do better.

Abraham Lincoln (1809–1865), President of the United States 1861–1865.

Jefferson Davis

He too, as President of the Confederate States, was also Commander-in-Chief of its armed forces. Unlike Lincoln, however, he had trained and served as a professional soldier. Born in Kentucky in 1808, he graduated from the United States Military Academy, West Point, and fought in several campaigns on the Western frontier before eloping in 1835 with the daughter of his commanding officer, the future President Zachary Taylor. He then settled on a plantation not far from Vicksburg and sat in the US Congress as a representative for Mississippi. In 1845 he resigned his seat in order to serve as colonel of the 1st Mississippi Rifles in the Mexican War, where he was wounded. He returned to Congress as senator for Mississippi, and was Secretary of War from 1853 to 1857. From then until 1861 he again served as

Jefferson Davis
(1808–1888),
President of the
Confederate States
1861–1865.

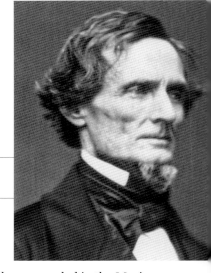

senator for Mississippi, becoming leader of the Southern Democrats and securing the passage of resolutions in defence of slavery. In January 1861 he was nominated provisional President of the newly formed Confederacy. He proved an inflexible figure in power and, like Lincoln, sometimes faced opposition from among his own people. Unlike him, Davis had enough military experience to feel justified in intervening at the operational level.

UNION GENERALS

Winfield Scott At the outbreak of the war, the General-in-Chief of the United States Army was Major General Winfield Scott, nicknamed 'Old Fuss and Feathers'. Born in Virginia in 1785, he had served in the War of 1812 and commanded in the Mexican War, but was by this time too old and ill for active service. Scarcely able to mount his horse and with a girth to match his great height, he was inclined to prefer the restaurant to the field and politics to active soldiering. When the question of secession arose, he recommended that the discontented States be allowed to leave in peace, but when hostilities began he stayed with the Union rather than his native State. Asked by Lincoln for a plan of action, he advocated a policy of economic warfare as a way of minimising bloodshed. The United States Navy, to be increased by a ship-building programme that the South could not match, would blockade the coast, while Union troops would march up the Mississippi from New Orleans, and down from Illinois, thus dividing the Confederacy in two. The great inland waterways as well as the oceans would thus be closed to contraband traffic and the South would eventually be forced to abandon the struggle.

Ultimately, this policy was the one carried into effect, but at the time it was ridiculed by wits as 'the Anaconda Plan', with cartoons showing a great Northern serpent attempting to surround and strangle the South. Public opinion on both sides wanted a war of movement that would bring hostilities to a rapid end. The cry in Washington was 'On to Richmond!' (the Confederate capital), while even cool heads argued that a long war, such as Scott's plan needed to become effective, would give the Confederates more time in which to seek international recognition. The British, whose mill-owners and workers in Lancashire were facing ruin, might send the Royal Navy to break the blockade, while the French, who had an army and puppet Emperor in Mexico, might also intervene. The first major action of the war, known as the First battle of Bull Run to the Union side and First Manassas to the Confederates, was fought on 21 July 1861. The shock of a totally unexpected defeat led to rapid and major changes in the Union forces. Major General George McClellan was given command of the Army of the Potomac, protecting Washington.

He became Lincoln's chief adviser on military matters and succeeded Scott as general-in-chief in November 1861.

Henry W. Halleck

In November 1861 the United States Army's Western Department, previously commanded by Major General John C. Frémont, was broken up to form the three new Military Departments of Kansas, New Mexico and the Missouri. Command of the latter went to Major General Henry Wager Halleck, born in New York in 1815 and a graduate of the USMA, West Point, who had served as an artillery officer in the Mexican and Black Hawk Wars. After resigning from the Army to practise as a lawyer in San Francisco, California, he continued to serve as a militia officer and gained a reputation for intellectual ability. He studied his military profession and was nick-named 'Old Brains', but he was criticised for undue caution as a field commander and for excessive centralisation after becoming general-in-chief in succession to McClellan in July 1862.

Ulysses S. Grant

In September 1861 command of the newly formed South-East District of Missouri, including southern Illinois, was assumed by Brigadier General Ulysses Simpson 'Sam' Grant. Born in Ohio in 1822, he was a former regular officer who had graduated from the USMA, West Point, and served with distinction in the Mexican War. Frustrated by subsequent garrison duty in the Far West and unable to keep his wife and small family on a captain's pay, he resigned his commission amid the allegations of intemperance that would dog him throughout his later years. After failing in various commercial ventures, he was found employment in his father's store in Galena, Illinois. When the Civil War began, he placed his sword at the disposal of the United States and spent the summer of 1861 training newly raised volunteers before being appointed colonel of the 21st Illinois Infantry. His promotion to brigadier general of Volunteers with command of a military district came as a surprise to him (his regimental uniform had not yet arrived from his tailor), but he wasted no time in moving to Cairo, Illinois, and taking up his new command. Originally part of Frémont's Western Department, it became a District of Halleck's Department of the Missouri when this was set up in November 1861.

Grant's first move was to seize Paducah, Kentucky, on 6 September 1861, so gaining control of the lower Ohio and its confluences with the Cumberland and the Tennessee. At the beginning of November 1861 he was ordered to move against Columbus, Kentucky, but finding the defences too strong, he landed on the opposite side of the Mississippi and captured the Confederate camp at Belmont on 7 November 1861. His success nearly turned to defeat when his inexperienced troops started to loot the abandoned enemy camp while the escorting gunboats, outgunned by the batteries at Columbus, retired up-river out of range. The Confederate commander, Leonidas Polk, a graduate of the USMA, West Point, and former Episcopalian Bishop of Louisiana, then ferried troops across the river from Columbus. Grant was hard put to re-embark his disorganised men and was himself almost left behind. With the Mississippi's banks made steeper by the low

Ulysses S. Grant (1822–1885) also served as President of the United States from 1869 to 1877.

autumn water-level, he escaped only by riding along a gang-plank hastily pushed out to him from one of the transports.

On 1 February 1862 Halleck approved Grant's proposal to attack Fort Henry, on the Cumberland, and Fort Donelson, twelve miles away overland, on the Tennessee. These positions, each about fifty miles upstream of the confluence of their respective rivers with the Ohio, had been established just inside the Tennessee State boundary, as a gesture towards Kentucky's claims of neutrality between North and South. Fort Henry was bombarded into surrender by Union gunboats on 6 February 1862. Grant, who had disembarked his 15,000 men to attack from the landward side and was still four miles away, turned to march on Fort Donelson. There the gunboats attacked on 14 February, but suffered severe damage and were forced to withdraw for repairs. Grant, left in the freezing cold without tents or other comforts for his men, feared that he would have to mount a regular siege. His position was much improved by the arrival of six gunboats and reinforcements from Fort Henry and Cairo.

The Confederate generals inside Donelson decided that their position was now untenable and, after a sortie on the night of 15 February, left the command to Brigadier General Simon Bolivar Buckner, a 48-year-old Kentuckian, who had served in the United States Infantry after graduating from the USMA, West Point. He had served alongside Grant in the Mexican War and was close enough to him to have paid Grant's hotel bill in New York, when Grant was on his way home after resigning from the Army. On 16 February he asked his old comrade for terms, but Grant realised that the Confederates themselves knew their position was hopeless and offered only 'unconditional and immediate surrender'. Buckner replied that this was 'ungenerous and unchivalrous', but was forced to accept them the same day. Grant nevertheless displayed his chivalry, and repaid Buckner's earlier generosity, by now placing his own purse at Buckner's disposal, knowing that, as a prisoner of war, it would be some time before he regained access to his own funds. Grant became the hero of the hour, the Northern newspapers making much of the initial letters of Unconditional Surrender being the same as those in his own name. Given command of the newly created District of West Tennessee, he was promoted major general of Volunteers on 16 February 1862.

The fall of the forts was followed by the advance of Grant's army, with two gunboats in support, to capture Nashville, the State capital of Tennessee, on 27 February. Halleck, however, rebuked Grant for going beyond the geographical limits of his command area and for refusing to send back troops as ordered. On 4 March he ordered Grant to hand over command to his senior divisional commander, Major General Charles F. Smith, a 60-year-old veteran who had been one of Grant's instructors at West Point. Grant complied, though he asked to be relieved of further duty under Halleck and thought seriously of resigning his commission. Halleck, having achieved command of the entire Western Department following Grant's capture of the two forts, restored him to his command and Grant took over from the dying Smith at Savannah, on the Tennessee, on 17 March.

Intending to attack the Confederates under General Albert Johnston at Corinth, Mississippi, Grant moved his own army of six divisions a few miles up-river to Pittsburg Landing. There, on 6 April 1862, Johnston pre-empted him with an attack on his unprepared camp. By the evening, General Pierre Beauregard, on whom the Confederate command devolved when Johnston was killed, was confident of victory. Artillery support from the gunboats and the arrival of reinforcements during the night turned the advantage to Grant. After fierce fighting during the following day (at its thickest around the church of Shiloh, from which the battle came to be named), Beauregard withdrew, leaving Grant in possession of the field.

Soon afterwards, Halleck joined the Army of the District of West Tennessee (formally re-designated the Army of the Tennessee on 21 April 1862) and advanced to Corinth, though his decision to entrench his camps at the end of each day's march so as to avoid another surprise attack gave the Confederates time to regroup. He then dispersed his forces along the southern boundary of Tennessee, from Memphis eastwards through Corinth and on to Chattanooga. In July 1862 he was called to Washington to replace McClellan. No one was appointed to fill his place as departmental commander, but in practice Grant was left as the senior officer in the Western theatre.

One of the formations under Grant's command was led by a prominent **John A. McClernand** Illinois lawyer and politician, John Alexander McClernand, born in Kentucky in 1812. A Democrat and former member of the US House of Representatives, he was both an opponent of the abolitionists and one of Lincoln's most valuable political allies in the Mid-West. With no military experience other than two months' service as a private soldier in the Illinois militia during the Black Hawk War, he was in Illinois when the war between the States began and became a leading figure in ensuring that Cairo, at the confluence of the Mississippi and the Ohio rivers, was held for the Union. In recognition of his success in raising recruits and his continued political support, Lincoln promoted him from colonel to brigadier general of Volunteers in August 1861, with seniority dating from the previous May. In October 1861, McClernand resigned from Congress in order to lead his troops in the field. He served under Grant at the capture of Fort Donelson, where his division bore the brunt of the Confederate sortie, and at Shiloh. On 21 March 1862 he was promoted by Lincoln to major general of Volunteers, the same rank that Grant himself held at that time, and junior to him by a mere few weeks.

William T. Sherman

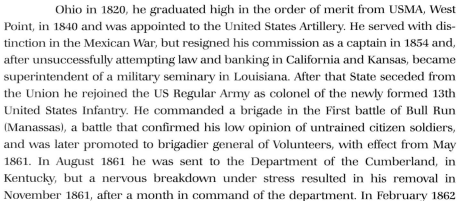

William Tecumseh Sherman (1820–1891), one of the most effective generals of the war, whose 'March to the Sea' in November–December 1864 was a decisive strategic blow to the Confederacy.

A more experienced general was William Tecumseh Sherman. Born in Ohio in 1820, he graduated high in the order of merit from USMA, West Point, in 1840 and was appointed to the United States Artillery. He served with distinction in the Mexican War, but resigned his commission as a captain in 1854 and, after unsuccessfully attempting law and banking in California and Kansas, became superintendent of a military seminary in Louisiana. After that State seceded from the Union he rejoined the US Regular Army as colonel of the newly formed 13th United States Infantry. He commanded a brigade in the First battle of Bull Run (Manassas), a battle that confirmed his low opinion of untrained citizen soldiers, and was later promoted to brigadier general of Volunteers, with effect from May 1861. In August 1861 he was sent to the Department of the Cumberland, in Kentucky, but a nervous breakdown under stress resulted in his removal in November 1861, after a month in command of the department. In February 1862 his old comrade and fellow-gunner, Halleck, at that time commanding the Department of the Missouri, gave him command of the District of Cairo, replacing Grant who had moved to the District of West Tennessee.

Sherman was promoted to major general of Volunteers on 1 May 1862 and, during Grant's campaign against Forts Henry and Donelson, was based at Paducah, with the task of forwarding supplies and reinforcements. The two generals established a firm mutual trust and friendship and Sherman readily waived his seniority as a regular officer in order to serve as one of Grant's divisional commanders. At Shiloh, he was the senior officer present before Grant arrived. When Halleck temporarily removed Grant from command, Sherman stood by him and was influential in persuading him not to resign.

Stephen A. Hurlbut

During the Vicksburg campaign, Grant relied on Major General Stephen Augustus Hurlbut for the protection of his bases and the steady flow of reinforcements and supplies. Born in South Carolina in 1815, Hurlbut first practised as a lawyer in Charleston, and served as adjutant of a Volunteer regiment during the Seminole War in Florida. In 1845 he moved to Illinois, where he entered politics and sat in the State legislature as a Republican. On the outbreak of the Civil War he was appointed a brigadier general of Volunteers and subsequently commanded a division at Shiloh and in the advance to Corinth. Hurlbut was promoted to major general of Volunteers in September 1862, with command first of XIII Corps and then, when it was formed in December 1862, XVI Corps. With his troops widely dispersed from Memphis along the northern borders of Tennessee, Hurlbut provided the cavalry whose raids distracted Confederate attention from Grant's passage of the Mississippi below Vicksburg.

In the final phase of the siege of Vicksburg, command of McClernand's XIII **Edward O. C. Ord**
Corps was transferred to Major General Edward Otho Cresap Ord. Born in
Maryland in 1818, he had studied at USMA, West Point, from which he graduated
with Grant in 1843. He was appointed to the United States Artillery, and served in
the Seminole and Mexican Wars and in expeditions against the Plains Indians.
During the early campaigns of the Civil War he had established a creditable record
as a general, both in Virginia and with the Army of the Tennessee, where he had
been wounded. Ord had long been on friendly terms with Grant, who compared
his military competence and unselfish nature favourably with that of McClernand.

Born in Ohio in 1828, James Birdseye McPherson passed out first in **James B. McPherson**
order of merit from the USMA, West Point, and was appointed to the
United States Engineers, with whom he served on the Atlantic and
Pacific coasts. He joined Halleck's staff in the Western theatre and was
Grant's chief engineer in the attack on Forts Henry and Donelson.
McPherson became a brigadier general of Volunteers in May 1862
and commanded the engineers of the Army of the Tennessee at
Shiloh, the advance to Corinth, and Iuka. In October 1862 he was promoted to major general of Volunteers, and led a wing of Grant's operations in northern Mississippi during December 1862 and January
1863. When Grant re-organised his army to renew the offensive
against Vicksburg, he recognised McPherson's ability as a field general by giving him command of the new XVII Corps.

THE CONFEDERATE GENERALS

The most senior Confederate general involved in the Vicksburg campaign **Joseph E. Johnston**
was Joseph Eggleston Johnston, born in 1807 into an aristocratic Virginia
family with a long tradition of military service. After graduating from the USMA,
West Point, he served in the United States Artillery and United States Corps of
Topographical Engineers and took part in the Seminole War in Florida and in the
Mexican War (where he was twice wounded), distinguishing himself in both campaigns. At the time of the outbreak of the War between the States he was a brigadier
general and Quartermaster General of the Army but, when Virginia seceded from
the Union, placed his sword at the disposal of his native State and became the high-
est-ranking officer of the US Army to join the Confederacy. Gracious and courteous
in manner and immaculate in appearance, he was the model of a Southern gentle-
man, well-liked by his subordinates, and popular with his men, who knew him as
'Little Joe' or 'the Gamecock', from his slight stature. He was, however, less admired
by his equals and superiors, who suffered from his punctilious regard for points of
military etiquette and for what he felt was due to him.

Joseph Eggleston Johnston (1807–1891) served as a congressman after the war and was an honorary pallbearer at Sherman's funeral.

After serving for a month as a major general of Virginia Volunteers, he was appointed a brigadier general in the regular Confederate States Army in May 1861 and was the senior Confederate officer present at the First battle of Bull Run (Manassas). In August 1861 he was one of the five officers promoted by Jefferson Davis to the rank of general in the Confederate States Army, all with seniority back-dated to 21 July, but placed in an order of precedence that made Johnston fourth of the five (Beauregard, the hero of Fort Sumter, who had served with him at Bull Run, was the only one ranked junior). To Johnston, who had relied upon the principle that officers would be ranked according to their former seniority in the US Army, this was both an injustice and an insult. He protested to Davis accordingly, implying that the President had been influenced by favouritism. Davis regarded his complaint as insubordinate and an estrangement grew between the two. He gave Johnston command of the Army of Northern Virginia in October 1861, but created further ill-feeling by subsequently criticising his strategy there.

At the Battle of Fair Oaks or Seven Pines, Virginia (31 May–1 June 1862) Johnston attacked McClellan's Army of the Potomac, but was wounded at a critical moment and the Union troops were able to maintain their position. Davis, present on the field, rode to Johnston's side and offered genuine sympathy, but when it became clear that Johnston would not be able to resume command, appointed General Robert E. Lee (one of the officers whom Johnston considered to have been wrongly given seniority over him) in his place. During his six months' convalescence in Richmond, Johnston saw Lee being given all the extra forces and resources for which he had asked in vain. Encouraged by some of his former comrades, he continued to nurse his grievances against Davis and the feud was taken up by their respective wives. Each presided over her own loyal circle of ladies and the refined atmosphere of polite Richmond society came to acquire distinct overtones of cat, with neither Lydia Johnston nor Varina Davis disposed to make up the quarrel, even if their husbands had been.

Nevertheless, Davis still respected Johnston as a seasoned veteran with experience of high command in the field. Under pressure from Johnston's friends in Congress, he selected him to command a newly created Department of the West, with authority over almost the entire Western theatre. Johnston's military authority would cover western North Carolina, northern Georgia, Tennessee, Alabama, Mississippi and Louisiana east of the great river. The troops at his disposal would include the Confederate forces around Vicksburg, under Lieutenant General John Pemberton, and the Army of Tennessee, under Lieutenant General Braxton Bragg, as well as formations holding Port Hudson on the Mississippi and Mobile on the coast of Alabama. Johnston established his new headquarters at Chattanooga,

Tennessee, in November 1862, but saw himself as an inspector-general and administrator rather than a commander. Unable, for political and logistic reasons, to unify his forces, or to make any changes in their senior officers, he argued that it was impossible for any general successfully to lead more than one army at a time and that even then the general could only do so when actually with it, not several hundred miles away.

At Vicksburg, command lay with Lieutenant General John Clifford Pemberton, born in Philadelphia, Pennsylvania, in 1814. After graduating from the USMA, West Point, he served with distinction in the United States Artillery in the Seminole and Mexican Wars, against the Plains Indians, and in the expedition against the Mormons who resisted the accession of Utah to the United States. At West Point and in his subsequent tours of garrison duty in the South, he made many Southern friends and came to share their views. He married a Southern lady twelve years his junior, Martha 'Patty' Thompson, of Norfolk, Virginia, diminutive of figure but determined of character. When her State left the Union he had no hesitation in resigning his commission as a captain in the 4th US Artillery, to become first a colonel of Virginia Volunteers and then a brigadier general in the Confederate States Army.

John C. Pemberton

After serving under Joseph E. Johnston in northern Virginia, he was posted to the Department of South Carolina, Georgia and Florida, where his experience with garrison artillery was specially valuable in preparing the coastal defences. He was promoted to major general, CSA, in January 1862, and succeeded Robert E. Lee as departmental commander there in March 1862. His inflexible Yankee ways (Grant, who had served with him in the Mexican War, described him with admiration as being 'scrupulously particular in matters of honour and integrity') and his strict prevention of unauthorised cotton exports made him unpopular with the businessmen of Charleston, South Carolina, who petitioned Jefferson Davis for the return of their original commander, General Pierre Beauregard. Davis had not been impressed by Beauregard's defeat at Shiloh in April 1862 and was glad of the opportunity to place him in a less active theatre.

In October 1862 Pemberton, promoted to lieutenant general, was given command of the Department of Mississippi and East Louisiana where the growing threat to Vicksburg seemed to call for an officer whose expertise lay in defensive warfare. He established his headquarters in Jackson and then took personal charge of improving the defences of Vicksburg, with forts and earthworks built to ring the city and new batteries deployed on the bluffs. His energy was much appreciated, but his Yankee birth made him an object of suspicion to many Mississippians, despite his being a

John C. Pemberton (1814–1881) was later suspected of treason because of his Northern birth, which led him to resign his commission. He was eventually recommissioned as a lieutenant colonel of artillery.

favourite of Mississippi's own Jefferson Davis. Charged by Davis with ensuring that Vicksburg did not fall, he knew that if he failed, not only would the South lose a vital strategic position, but that Davis' own judgement would be called into question, for having entrusted such an important post to someone who had been born a Yankee.

Martin L. Smith At the time of the first Union attack on Vicksburg the defences were under Brigadier General Martin Luther Smith, who assumed command shortly before Flag Officer Farragut and his naval squadron arrived from New Orleans. Born in New York in 1819, he graduated from the USMA, West Point, and served in the US Corps of Topographical Engineers, mostly in the Southern States. Sympathising with the South, he resigned his US Army captaincy on the outbreak of the Civil War and joined the Confederate States Engineers. He then became colonel of the 21st Louisiana Infantry at New Orleans, with promotion to brigadier general a few days before the city fell to Farragut on 24 April 1862. He was then posted to Vicksburg, where he arrived on 12 May and speeded the construction of defence works, installing eighteen heavy guns in eight batteries high on the bluffs, sited to control the river. In contrast with the suspicion accorded to Pemberton, his Yankee origins were never held against him and his stern, decisive, taciturn manner inspired confidence among soldiers and citizens alike. As the size and importance of the Confederate forces around Vicksburg grew, Smith became one of Pemberton's divisional commanders, with promotion to major general on 4 November 1862.

THE UNION NAVAL AND MARINE OFFICERS

David D. Porter Son of the captain of the famous USS *Essex* in the War of 1812, he was born in 1813 and began his career with the United States Navy at the age of eleven. He

took part in anti-piracy operations in the West Indies under his father's command and subsequently served with him from 1826 to 1829 in the Mexican Navy. He then rejoined the US Navy and became an experienced sea officer, with active service during the Mexican War to his credit. In April 1861, at the beginning of the Civil War, he was promoted to commander and assigned to the 11-gun steamer *Powhatan* in the Gulf Blockading Squadron under Flag Officer William W. McKean. The blockade deterred ordinary merchantmen, but failed to stop Confederate commerce raiders and privateers. Worse still for the prestige of the US Navy, on 12 October 1861 a detachment of four Union ships was driven away from the Heads of the Passes, in the Mississippi estuary. USS *Richmond* was rammed by the converted river-steamer CSS *Manassas* and ran aground, while USS *Vincennes* also ran aground and was temporarily abandoned in a panic before the entire force retreated downstream to avoid Confederate fire-rafts.

Much of the panic was the result of psychological warfare by the Confederate Commodore George N. Hollins, a former captain in the United States Navy, born in 1799. A veteran of the War of 1812 and operations against pirates in the Mediterranean, he resigned his commission to join the Confederacy and achieved his first success in Chesapeake Bay on 29 June 1861. There, after taking passage in the steamer *St Nicholas* disguised as a woman, he seized the ship in the early hours of the morning and took her into Confederate waters. Since reaching New Orleans, he had been curdling the blood of the blockading squadron with stories of new inventions in naval warfare, steam rams, torpedoes (mines) and similar devices.

In November 1861, Porter visited Gideon Welles, Lincoln's Secretary of the Navy, with a plan to capture New Orleans by an amphibious operation. Welles took him to see Lincoln, who was attracted by the idea and called in McClellan, his chief military adviser. As Porter later remembered, Lincoln stressed that the expedition should have enough troops not only to take New Orleans, but to press on to Vicksburg, describing it as 'the key to all that country watered by the Mississippi and its tributaries'. Pointing to the map, he said 'See what a lot of land these fellows hold, of which Vicksburg is the key. I am acquainted with that region and know what I am talking about. It means hog and hominy without limit, fresh troops from all the States of the Far South, and a cotton country where they can raise the staple without interference. Valuable as New Orleans will be to us, Vicksburg will be even more so … the war can never be brought to a close until that key is in our pocket.' Porter was asked whom he would recommend to command the naval element of the expedition and recommended his foster-brother, Captain David Farragut.

David Glasgow Farragut, born in Tennessee in 1801, had grown up as a member of the family of his father's close friend, Captain David Porter of the USS *Essex*. Farragut became a midshipman in the US Navy at the age of nine and served under Captain Porter during the War of 1812. He later saw service in the West Indies and the Mediterranean and was promoted to captain in 1855. Without a ship at the beginning of the Civil War, he readily accepted command of the Western Gulf Blockading Squadron, with the capture of New Orleans as his most important task. Like most naval officers, he knew the city and its approaches well, and believed that it could be taken from the sea. With the steam-sloop *Hartford* as his flagship, he reached Ship Island in the estuary of the Mississippi on 20 February 1862. From there, with a total of seventeen seagoing warships and nineteen mortar schooners, complete with steam tugs, he prepared for the attack on New Orleans.

David G. Farragut

Andrew H. Foote   On 5 September 1861 command of the Union gunboats on the upper Mississippi was assumed by Captain (Commodore) Andrew Hull Foote. Born in Connecticut in 1806, he was for a short time a cadet at the USMA, West Point, before joining the US Navy as a midshipman. A zealous evangelical who preached to his crews every Sunday and banned alcohol from his ships, he had served against pirates in the East Indies, the Chinese off Canton and slave-traders off the West Coast of Africa. At the outbreak of the Civil War he had been in charge of the Navy Yard at Brooklyn, New York. After arriving at Cairo, Illinois, he pressed on with the completion of the river flotilla begun under Commander John Rodgers and established cordial personal relations with Grant, under whose orders he was to operate. In November 1861 he sent two gunboats to support Grant at Belmont and in February 1862 led his flotilla in the attacks on Forts Henry and Donelson, where he was wounded. He remained in command for the capture of Island No.10 (the chartmakers' name for the tenth major island up-river from the sea) and New Madrid, Missouri, early in April, but, with his wounds slow to heal, was relieved on medical grounds at his own request.

Charles H. Davis   Foote's successor was Commodore Charles Henry Davis, born in Massachusetts in 1807. After thirty years in the US Navy he became a commander in 1854 and was promoted to captain in November 1861. After commanding the South Atlantic Blockading Squadron during the winter of 1861–62, he was assigned to the Navy Department in Washington, from where he joined the Upper Mississippi flotilla at the beginning of May 1862. After a number of successful engagements, he joined Farragut's squadron at Vicksburg on 1 July 1862 and supported his operations until both formations were compelled to retire at the end of the month. In September 1862 he became chief of the Bureau of Navigation at the Navy Department, and command of the flotilla was assumed by David D. Porter, newly promoted to acting rear-admiral.

Samuel Phillips Lee   One of Farragut's most adventurous officers was Commander S. P. Lee. Born in 1812, he was a member of the same aristocratic Virginian family that produced 'Light Horse Harry' Lee in the American War of Independence and Robert E. Lee in the War between the States. He entered the US Navy in 1827 and served on various stations round the world. At an early stage in his career, in the Pacific, he proved a difficult subordinate and was suspended from duty as first lieutenant of the USS *Peacock*. He fought two duels, and killed a fellow-passenger on a Mississippi steamboat. After a tour with the Coast Survey, he served in the Mexican War in command of the USS *Washington*. He was subsequently employed on hydrographic duties before being given command of the USS *Vandalia* with orders to join the United States Eastern Fleet. On reaching Cape Town he heard that Fort Sumter had been fired upon and, on his own initiative, returned to the USA. He remained loyal to the Union and was immediately employed on blockade duty. Early in 1862 he was given command of the full-rigged steam sloop USS *Oneida*, assigned to Farragut's Western Gulf Blockading Squadron.

Apart from the detachments embarked in Farragut's warships, the United States **Charles Ellet, Jr** Marine Corps was not employed in the Mississippi campaign. Their place was filled by the Mississippi Marine Brigade under members of the Ellet family. This formation was raised by Charles Ellet, Jr, a Pennsylvanian by birth and a civil engineer by profession, who had spent the years before the war in Illinois, working on bridges, locks and dams. He persuaded Edwin Stanton, Lincoln's Secretary of War, that a ram fleet would perform valuable service on the great western rivers and was accordingly authorised to form one. Finding numerous river steamers laid up on account of the war, he converted several of them to rams by adding heavy timbers fore and aft, installing sharp metal beaks at the prow, and rebuilding their engines to give a speed of fifteen knots. In late April 1862 he was given command of them, with a commission for himself as colonel, and for his brother, Alfred Washington Ellet (who had also been a civil engineer in Illinois and who was at this time a captain in the 59th Illinois Infantry) as lieutenant colonel and second in command. Each of the nine rams was commanded by a member of his family.

This force, which became the Mississippi Marine Brigade, was raised as United States Volunteers, part neither of the regular US Army nor the Volunteers provided by the various States, whose contingents made up the greater part of the Union armies. Carried aboard the rams, the brigade's infantrymen could take part in combat from the deck, or disembark for operations ashore in much the same way as the marines of a seagoing fleet. The force was not assigned to any of the local army commanders, but came under the US Navy for operational purposes. Like their comrades in the river gunboats, the complements of the Ellet rams suffered from all the disadvantages of their environment, including clouds of biting insects in warm weather, with clammy mists and dampness in winter changing to extreme heat in the summer, especially when the boilers were fired up. In addition, they were prey to the various diseases that resulted from their reliance on the river itself for most of their drinking-water. Nevertheless, despite the political problems arising from being 'Nobody's Own', Ellet's brigade was proud of its special role as a water-borne formation and resisted all attempts to bring it into line with the rest of the Army.

THE CONFEDERATE NAVAL OFFICERS

The Confederate side included many former officers of the United **James E. Montgomery** States Navy, but few with an interest in fighting a war on the inland rivers. This was left to individuals such as James Ed Montgomery, born in Kentucky in 1817, and a steamboat operator by profession. He persuaded the Confederate Congress to allot one million dollars for the purchase of fourteen river steamers and their conversion to rams, each armed with a single heavy gun and protected by cotton bales. These vessels, forming the River Defense Fleet, were intended primarily for the protection of New Orleans and were crewed by river boatmen under the Confederate War Department, rather than by the Confederate Navy. Most of them were lost when Farragut captured New Orleans, but the eight rams of the upper division had previously been sent upstream and, under Commodore Montgomery's command, saw service against Union gunboats coming down the Mississippi. The individualist ways of Montgomery's river-boat captains incurred the scorn of the Confederacy's professional naval officers, who pointed out the tactical short-comings of commanders who had never been trained to manoeuvre in a disciplined fleet action.

Issac N. Brown   Greater success was achieved by Lieutenant Isaac Newton Brown, born in Kentucky in 1817. With twenty-seven years to his credit as an officer in the United States Navy, including active duty during the Mexican War, he resigned his commission when his ship returned home after the outbreak of the Civil War and in June 1861 was appointed a lieutenant in the Confederate States Navy. After acting as an adviser to the Army in the construction of river defences on the Mississippi and the Cumberland, he was given the task of supervising the building of four ironclads at New Orleans, but the city fell before they could be completed. He was subsequently ordered to Vicksburg and appointed to the ram *Arkansas*, lying in the upper reaches of the Yazoo. When eventually brought into commission by Brown, she challenged the combination of Farragut's sea-going warships and Davis' river gunboats above Vicksburg.

THE ARMIES

The armies on both sides consisted predominantly of citizen soldiers who had responded to the call of their respective governments for volunteers. Few had any experience of army service and even the militia on which the United States had for generations relied was little more than a series of military clubs. Most regimental officers were as ignorant of their duties as their men, with colonels appointed by State governors as much from their political influence as their command skills, and captains elected by the men of the companies they led. On the Union side, the professional soldiers of the small regular army were for the most part retained in their existing units. On the Confederate side, because there was no pre-existing regular army, those professional soldiers who resigned from the United States Army (or deserted from it, in the case of enlisted men) were available as cadres around which Volunteer regiments could form. Both sides used the same drill-books and manuals, which officers and sergeants had to learn, together with every other aspect of their duties, as they went along. These reflected the tactical requirements derived from the smooth-bore muzzle-loading flintlock firearms of the Napoleonic period, the last great conflict of European warfare. In fact, during the decade preceding the

Civil War, armies had begun to re-arm with rifled percussion muskets, giving a greater range, accuracy and reliability that made attacks by densely formed columns of infantry much less likely to succeed. Most of the senior generals on both sides had been trained at the same US Military Academy, West Point, where the Napoleonic principles of the spirited offensive had been taught. A good number had fought on the same side as young officers in the Mexican War, where the abandonment of positions by Mexican troops before the glittering bayonets of the charging 'Gringo' infantry seemed to bear out the theories that they had been taught.

The Army of the Tennessee changed its composition and organisation as well as its name during the operations leading to the advance on Vicksburg. When Grant at last crossed the Mississippi at the end of April 1863, it consisted of four Corps, of which three (XIII, XV and XVII) were with him in the field, and the fourth (XVI, under Major General Stephen A. Hurlbut) remained holding the line eastwards from Memphis through northern Tennessee.

THE ORDERS OF BATTLE

All the regiments listed below are infantry unless shown otherwise. Volunteer regiments are listed alphabetically, by State.

THE ARMY OF THE TENNESSEE (Major General Ulysses S Grant)
Company 'A', 4th Illinois Cavalry
1st Battalion, The Engineer Regiment of the West

XIII CORPS (Major General John A. McClernand, succeeded by Major General
  Edward O. C. Ord, 19 June 1863)
  Company 'L', 3rd Illinois Cavalry
  Independent Pioneer Company, Kentucky Infantry
Ninth Division (Brigadier General Peter J. Osterhaus)
  2nd, 3rd Illinois Cavalry; 6th Missouri Cavalry
  7th Battery, Michigan Light Artillery; 1st Battery, Wisconsin Light Artillery
  1st Brigade: 118th Illinois; 49th, 69th Indiana; 7th Kentucky; 120th Ohio
  2nd Brigade: 54th Indiana; 22nd Kentucky; 16th, 42nd, 114th Ohio
Tenth Division (Brigadier General Andrew A. Smith)
  Company 'C', 4th Indiana Cavalry
  Chicago Mercantile Battery, Illinois Light Artillery; 17th Battery, Ohio Light
  Artillery
  1st Brigade: 16th, 60th, 67th Indiana; 83rd, 96th Ohio; 23rd Wisconsin
  2nd Brigade: 77th, 97th, 130th Illinois; 19th Kentucky; 48th Ohio
Twelfth Division (Brigadier General Alvin P. Hovey)
  Company 'C', 1st Indiana Cavalry
  Battery 'A', 1st Missouri Light Artillery; 2nd, 16th Batteries, Ohio Light Artillery
  1st Brigade: 11th, 24th, 34th, 46th Indiana; 29th Wisconsin
  2nd Brigade: 87th Illinois; 47th Indiana; 24th, 28th Iowa; 56th Ohio

Fourteenth Division (Brigadier General Eugene A. Carr)
Company 'G', 3rd Illinois Cavalry
Siege Train, 1st US Artillery; Battery 'A', 2nd Illinois Light Artillery; 1st Battery,
   Indiana Light Artillery
1st Brigade: 33rd, 99th Illinois; 8th, 18th Indiana
2nd Brigade: 21st, 22nd, 23rd Iowa; 11th Wisconsin

XV CORPS (Major General William T. Sherman)
4th Iowa Cavalry
First Division (Major General Frederick Steele)
Kane County Independent Company, Illinois Cavalry; Company 'D', 3rd Illinois
   Cavalry
1st Battery, Iowa Light Artillery; Battery 'F', 2nd Missouri Light Artillery; 4th
   Battery, Ohio Light Artillery
1st Brigade: 13th Illinois; 27th, 29th, 30th, 31st, 32nd Missouri
2nd Brigade: 25th, 31st Iowa; 3rd, 12th, 17th Missouri; 76th Ohio
3rd Brigade: 4th, 9th, 26th, 30th Iowa
Second Division (Major General Frank F. Blair)
Companies 'A', 'B', Thielemann's Battalion, Illinois Cavalry; Company 'C', 10th
   Missouri Cavalry
Batteries 'A', 'B', 'H', 1st Illinois Light Artillery; 8th Battery, Ohio Light Artillery
1st Brigade: 13th US Infantry; 113th, 116th Illinois; 6th, 8th Missouri
2nd Brigade: 55th, 127th Illinois; 83rd Indiana; 54th, 57th Ohio
3rd Brigade: 30th, 37th, 47th Ohio; 4th West Virginia.
Third Division (Brigadier General James M. Tuttle)
Battery 'E', 1st Illinois Light Artillery; 2nd Battery, Iowa Light Artillery
1st Brigade: 114th Illinois; 93rd Indiana; 72nd, 95th Ohio
2nd Brigade: 47th Illinois; 5th Minnesota; 11th Missouri; 8th Wisconsin
3rd Brigade: 8th, 12th, 35th Iowa

XVII CORPS (Major General James B. McPherson)
4th Company, Ohio Cavalry
Third Division (Major General John A. Logan)
Company 'A', 2nd Illinois Cavalry
Battery 'D', 1st Illinois Light Artillery; Batteries 'G', 'L', 2nd Illinois Light Artillery;
8th Battery, Michigan Light Artillery; 3rd Battery, Ohio Light Artillery
1st Brigade: 20th, 35th, 45th, 124th Illinois; 23rd Indiana
2nd Brigade: 30th Illinois; 20th, 68th, 78th Ohio
3rd Brigade: 8th, 17th, 81st Illinois; 7th Missouri; 32nd Ohio
Sixth Division (Brigadier General John McArthur)
Company 'G', 11th Illinois Cavalry
Battery 'F', 2nd Illinois Light Artillery; 1st Battery, Minnesota Light Artillery;
Battery 'C', 1st Missouri Light Artillery; 10th Battery, Ohio Light Artillery

1st Brigade: 1st Kansas; 16th Wisconsin

2nd Brigade: 11th, 72nd, 95th Illinois; 14th, 17th Wisconsin

3rd Brigade: 11th, 13th, 15th, 16th Iowa

Seventh Division (Brigadier General Isaac F. Quinby, succeeded by Brigadier
  General John E. Smith, 3 June 1863)

  Company 'F', 4th Missouri Cavalry

  Battery 'M', 1st Missouri Light Artillery; 11th Battery, Ohio Light Artillery;
  6th, 12th Batteries, Wisconsin Light Artillery

  1st Brigade: 48th, 59th Indiana; 4th Minnesota; 18th Wisconsin

  2nd Brigade: 56th Illinois; 17th Iowa; 10th, 24th Missouri; 80th Ohio

  3rd Brigade: 93rd Illinois; 5th, 10th Iowa; 26th Missouri

These were the three Corps with which Grant crossed the Mississippi at the end of
April 1863 and subsequently gained the battles that led to his investment of
Vicksburg. After the beginning of the siege, the troops there were joined during late
May and early June by a division under Major General Francis J. Herron, made up
of three regiments of cavalry and eight of infantry from the Department of the
Missouri, and by three divisions from XVI Corps, under the command of Major
General Cadwallader C. Washburn. In mid-June, IX Corps, under Major General
John G. Parke, arrived after being transferred from Major General Ambrose E.
Burnside's Army of the Ohio.

  To guard the west side of the Mississippi, Grant established a District of North-
East Louisiana under Brigadier General Elias S. Dennis, with a mixed brigade made
up of Companies 'A', 'D', 'G' and 'K', 10th Illinois Cavalry, and the 63rd, 108th, 120th
and 131st Illinois Infantry. Six regiments of the newly formed 'African Brigade' (the
8th, 9th, 11th and 13th Louisiana Colored Infantry and the 1st and 3rd Mississippi
Colored Infantry) were assigned to the defence of the logistic base at Milliken's
Bend, on the Mississippi just above Vicksburg, with the 1st Arkansas Colored
Infantry and 10th Louisiana Colored Infantry at Goodrich's Landing.

A photograph, in the album of Surgeon Bixby of the Union hospital ship *Red Rover*, taken from the western bank of the Mississippi as Union artillery pounded Vicksburg.

The Confederate force opposed to Grant in the defence of Vicksburg was the army of the Department of Mississippi and East Louisiana, under Lieutenant General John C. Pemberton. Its main force consisted of five infantry divisions, organised as shown below (artillery and engineers not listed):

First Division (Major General William W. Loring)

  1st Brigade: 6th, 15th, 20th, 23rd, 26th Mississippi

  2nd Brigade: 1st, 3rd, 22nd, 31st, 33rd Mississippi

  3rd Brigade: 27th, 35th, 54th, 55th Alabama; 9th Arkansas; 3rd, 7th Kentucky; 12th Louisiana

Stevenson's Division (Major General Carter L. Stevenson)

  1st Brigade: 40th, 41st, 42nd, 43rd, 52nd Georgia

  2nd Brigade: 20th, 23rd, 30th, 31st, 46th Alabama

  3rd Brigade: 34th, 36th, 39th, 56th, 57th Georgia

  4th Brigade: 3rd, 31st, 43rd, 59th Tennessee; Texas Legion

Forney's Division (Major General John H. Forney)

  Hebert's Brigade: 2nd Alabama; 3rd, 21st Louisiana; 7th, 36th, 37th, 38th, 43rd Mississippi

  Moore's Brigade: 37th, 40th, 42nd Alabama; 1st, 35th, 40th Mississippi;2nd Texas

Smith's Division (Major General Martin L. Smith)

  1st Brigade: 17th, 31st Louisiana; 4th, 46th Mississippi

  Vaughn's Brigade: 60th, 61st, 62nd Tennessee

  3rd Brigade: 26th, 27th, 28th Louisiana; Mississippi State Troops

Bowen's Division (Major General John S. Bowen)

  3rd Missouri Cavalry

  1st (Missouri) Brigade: 1st/4th, 2nd, 3rd, 5th, 6th Missouri

  2nd Brigade: 1st, 12th, 15th, 19th, 20th, 21st Arkansas

Unattached: 10th Alabama Cavalry (Col. Wirt Adams); 10th Arkansas Cavalry (Col. C. R. Barteau)

General Joseph E. Johnston, commanding the Department of the West, took personal command of the operations around Vicksburg on 13 May 1863. At Jackson, he found two brigades (Gregg's, from Port Hudson on the Mississippi, and Walker's, from Beauregard's Department of South Carolina and Georgia) that had arrived too late to combine with Pemberton's field army. A week later, Johnston was joined by Gist's Brigade, from Beauregard's Department, and Ector's and McNair's Brigades from Bragg's Army of Tennessee. These were followed by Loring's 1st Division, which had become separated from Pemberton during the Confederate retreat to Vicksburg, and by Maxey's Brigade from Port Hudson. Additional reinforcements included Breckenridge's Division and Evans' Brigade from South Carolina, together with Jackson's cavalry brigade from the Army of Tennessee. Pemberton's cavalry remained in the field after his withdrawal within the defences of Vicksburg and, like Loring, thereafter came under Johnston's direct command.

UNIFORMS AND WEAPONS

In silhouette, there was little to differentiate the soldiers of the opposing armies, both of which drew on the same military traditions. The standard head-dress was a French-style *kepi*, as worn by most other Western armies of the period, but with a lower crown. This alternated with a broad-brimmed felt hat, more often (though not invariably) worn by officers and mounted men. Troops wore either a hip-length jacket or full-skirted tunic. Union troops wore the dark-blue coat and French-grey nether garments of the pre-war United States Army. The Confederates wore grey uniforms, though as stocks of cloth and dyestuffs ran low, many turned to locally produced material in 'butternut', a light-brown colour. Both sides affected the same 'facing colours' to distinguish the various arms; yellow for cavalry; red for artillery and engineers and light-blue for the infantry.

Infantry units of both armies were normally armed with a muzzle-loading percussion-lock rifled musket, with a long, narrow, triangular-section bayonet. Different patterns, calibres and makes of musket were in use, reflecting the problems of hastily raised mass armies. The 1855 Springfield musket was the standard-issue infantry weapon of the US Army, but the Western theatre had low priority and many of Grant's regiments were equipped with old flintlock smooth-bores that had been converted to percussion rifles, or with Belgian weapons, imported at the beginning of the war, that were almost as dangerous to the person firing as to the one aimed at. The variety of calibres made ammunition supply a problem, especially in a heated engagement, when men could fire up to three rounds a minute, and empty their pouches in an hour. At Vicksburg, the Confederate infantry had ample stocks of Enfield percussion rifles, brought in by British blockade-runners, or, as the US Navy Department indignantly described them, 'English pirates'. Cavalry on both sides (to the scorn of European military observers) tended to fight as mounted infantry, using their carbines, or with revolvers rather than swords. Nevertheless, many cavalrymen carried swords, as did officers of all arms.

Field artillery units (termed light artillery by the US Army of the day) were commonly equipped with the 1857-pattern smooth-bore muzzle-loading 12pdr gun, turned into a four-wheeled vehicle by the addition of a limber and a team of four horses. With a range of up to 2,000 yards, it could fire solid shot, explosive shells, or canister for local defence. For the first few rounds, a well-trained detachment could shoot almost as quickly as an infantryman could fire his musket, but the labour of running the gun back to its original platform after recoil meant that this rate was impossible to maintain. The 32-pdr siege guns, of which Grant's army had the only battery in the West, relied not on speed of action, but on absolute, steady, continuous accuracy. At Vicksburg, the Confederate shore batteries had a variety of heavy guns, including 50-pdr rifled cannon and 8in smooth-bores, with which to oppose the Union's ironclad gunboats. One of their large cannon was known to both sides as 'Whistling Dick', from the distinctive sound of its projectiles.

RIVER WARFARE
THE RIVER ROADS TO VICKSBURG

THE DESCENT TO NEW MADRID: MARCH – APRIL 1862

At the beginning of the War between the States, the United States Navy consisted of forty-two major combatant sailing vessels, twenty-six of them with auxiliary steam engines, carrying between them 555 guns and 7,600 officers and men. With its heaviest units consisting of frigates and sloops, it was essentially a blue-water navy, primarily intended for the protection of the nation's far-reaching merchant fleet and the disruption of enemy sea-borne trade in time of war. About a quarter of them were deployed in support of the multi-national effort to stamp out the African slave trade. Although in carrying out these roles the US Navy, like its European counterparts, might function from time to time as a brown-water navy, taking its ships into creeks, estuaries and the navigable rivers that emptied into them, not one of its warships was designed for service on the great inland waterways of the North American continent.

There, by the summer of 1861, the lower Mississippi was held by Confederate positions at Columbus, Kentucky; Island No 10 above New Madrid, Missouri; Fort Pillow at Memphis, Tennessee; Vicksburg; Grand Gulf; Port Hudson and finally, by the seaward defences of New Orleans itself. Among its major tributaries, the southwestern stretches of the Ohio were well within reach of Confederate raiders. Aided by local sympathisers, Confederate horse artillery might prevent the movement of steamboats carrying Federal troops and cargoes, while Confederate cavalry harassed the river ports. Some Federal strategists feared that, at worst, a Confederate army might carry the war up the Ohio into Pennsylvania, or at least stand upon the river and so prevent Kentucky and Tennessee from coming under Federal control. All the steamboats on Southern waterways were available to the Confederates for the transport of men and supplies, and the more powerful could be strengthened and armed as gunboats or rams.

Gaining control of these rivers was an essential element in Federal strategy. With the Mississippi closed, the Mid-West was denied its southward access to the sea. The only alternative trade-route was via the Great Lakes and the Northern railways, where freight rates rose to meet the increased demand. Just as the US Navy blockaded the Confederate coast, so the Confederate shore batteries blockaded the Union's most vital inland waterway. There was a possibility that prolonged closure might lead the Mid-Western states to disregard the issues both of slavery and the preservation of the Union and make their own peace with the Confederacy. At the operational level, no Federal army could enter Tennessee from the north without being able to rely on the rivers for transport. There was only one railway running south from the Ohio through Kentucky into Tennessee, and this was vulnerable to sabotage by Confederate supporters. Without control of the rivers, an army invading the South from Illinois, Indiana or Ohio risked

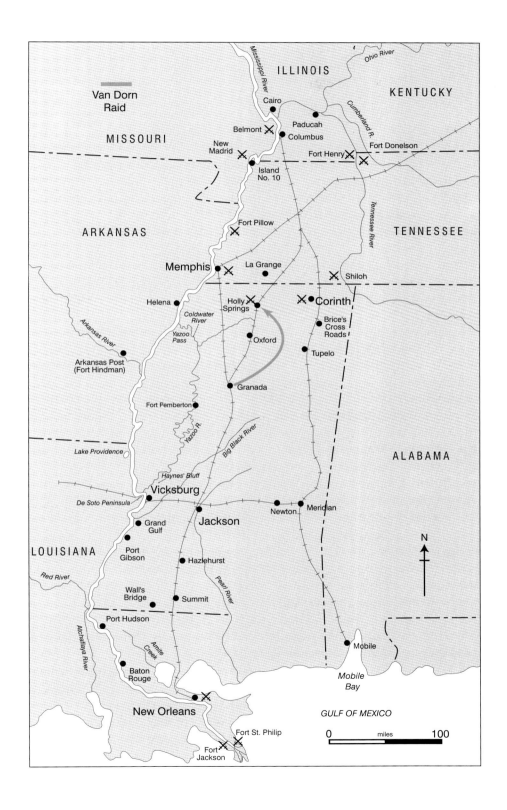

Van Dorn
Raid

ILLINOIS

KENTUCKY

Mississippi River

Ohio River

Cairo

Cumberland R.

MISSOURI

Belmont ✕
Paducah
Columbus

New
Madrid ✕

Fort Henry ✕✕

Fort Donelson ✕

Island
No. 10

Tennessee River

TENNESSEE

ARKANSAS

Fort Pillow ✕

Memphis ✕
La Grange

Shiloh ✕

Helena
*Coldwater
River*

Holly ✕
Springs

✕ Corinth

*Yazoo
Pass*

Brice's
Cross
Roads

Arkansas River

Oxford

Tupelo

Arkansas Post
(Fort Hindman)

Granada

Fort Pemberton

Yazoo R.

ALABAMA

Big Black River

Lake Providence

Haynes' Bluff

Vicksburg

De Soto Peninsula

Newton
Meridian

Jackson

Grand
Gulf

LOUISIANA

Port
Gibson

Hazlehurst

Red River

Pearl River

Wall's
Bridge
Summit

Port Hudson

Atchafalaya River

*Amite
Creek*

Mobile

Baton
Rouge

N

*Mobile
Bay*

New Orleans

✕

GULF OF MEXICO

Fort St. Philip

Fort ✕✕
Jackson

0   miles   100

35

defeat far from its bases, and the uncovering of these States to a Confederate counter-attack.

Given the strength of the Confederate defences, it soon became clear that the Union forces needed not just transport steamers to move and supply their armies, but a completely new type of war vessel, the armoured river gunboat, able to engage shore batteries on equal terms. The first three, *Conestoga*, *Tyler* and *Lexington*, were side-wheel paddle steamers, which before the war had carried freight and passengers as ordinary merchant river-boats. During May and June 1861, at Cincinnati, they were converted to a war role by the addition of guns, extra coal-bunkers and oak bulwarks such as protected seagoing warships of the time, thick enough to withstand shot from smooth-bore artillery. They started down-river in July, but, at a time of low water, constantly grounded on the bars of the Ohio and did not reach Cairo, on the Mississippi, until 1 September.

They were soon joined by a class of specially designed gunboats, of which the first to be commissioned was *St Louis*, later renamed *Baron de Kalb* as there was already a 20-gun sloop *St Louis* in the US Navy. With her consorts *Carondelet*, *Cincinnati*, *Louisville*, *Mound City*, *Cairo* and *Pittsburg*, she was built on the Mississippi at St Louis, Missouri, during October 1861. With a complement of seven officers and some 150 men, each measured 175 feet long and 52 feet wide, displaced some 600 tons and drew six feet of water when fully laden, and had a maximum speed of nine knots. The gun-deck, about a foot above the water-line of the wooden hull, was protected at the sides, bow and stern, by a casemate, inclined inboard at an angle of thirty-five degrees and armoured with iron plates 2½ inches thick. Three heavy guns, normally including the 'Parrott guns' (large rifled cannon devised by the ordnance expert Robert Parrott of New York), were fitted in the bow, and four along each side. The casemate also protected the engines and boilers and the single stern-wheel, with the pilot-house and twin smoke-stacks projecting above the main casemate. These ironclads were designed and built by James B. Eads, of St Louis, who from humble origins had risen to head his own firm as a river-boat builder and salvage-contractor for boats and cargoes sunk in the Western rivers. The delay of the US War Department in settling his bills meant that when his ironclads first went into action they were technically still his private property.

These boats formed the nucleus of a river navy that by the end of the war would have about one hundred armed steamers in commission. They were soon joined by two existing larger wooden boats, *Essex* and *Benton*, converted to heavy gunboats by the addition of cannon and stout defences. A year later they would be joined by another class of warship, known as tinclads, converted transports fitted with light armour against musketry, but able to navigate in much shallower waters than the heavy wood and ironclads. All these vessels were driven by the coal-burning steam-engines of the period, generating plumes of white steam and clouds of black smoke, with the reliability of the boilers always a cause of anxiety. In support, a flotilla of thirty-eight mortar-vessels was commissioned, consisting of open-topped barges with high bulwarks around a single large piece of ordnance.

Lacking sails or engines, they were towed from place to place by unarmoured tugs.

On the Mississippi, the Confederates abandoned their defences at Columbus and fell back forty miles downstream to New Madrid. This was occupied from the landward side by Union troops on 14 March 1862, but with Confederate batteries dominating the river from Island No 10, no Union vessels could pass. Flag Officer Foote, commanding the Union flotilla from the wooden gunboat *Benton*, was reluctant to make the attempt, as the Eads gunboats, despite their notional design speed, had proved under-powered for the fast Mississippi currents. With the river in full spate, any damage to their engines or steering gear would result in the boats becoming uncontrollable and being swept rapidly downstream to make easy targets for the Confederate gunners. If they were to be sunk, or destroyed after running aground, the whole strategic balance might change. Foote's fear was that the Confederate flotilla above Memphis might overwhelm his surviving vessels and then dash up the Mississippi to raid St Louis, or up the Ohio to Cincinnati, cutting the Union Army's supply lines in the process. In particular, he was concerned about the ram *Manassas*, believed to be at Memphis, and the 4,000-ton iron-clad *Louisiana*, then under construction at New Orleans. If that ship came up-river with her sixteen heavy guns, she would outmatch any vessel in the Union flotilla.

It was decided therefore to by-pass Island No.10 by making a channel through a series of swamps and bayous on the western side of the Mississippi and rejoining the river at New Madrid. Apart from moving the earth for a cut fifty feet wide and four feet deep, the Union engineers and their working parties of soldiers and sailors had to clear a way through numerous fallen logs and stumps of great trees, many of them submerged by the chilly water that the cut's excavation let into the swamp. Much of the work had to be done with hand tools, but steam-power and capstans from the advancing boats were used to drag out the heavy trunks and roots, and special saws were rigged to cut down any trees left in the water to four feet below the surface. After nineteen days of cutting, digging, dredging and hauling, the channel was opened and, at the end of March 1862, a little flotilla of steamboats came out of the forest to join the army at New Madrid. When Major General John Pope, the local army commander, asked for the support of a heavier gunboat, Commander Henry Walke of the *Carondelet* volunteered to run the batteries to join them.

During the night of 4 April *Carondelet*, fitted with extra defences consisting of chains, hawsers, cordwood and planking, and with one barge stacked with hay-bales lashed along the side nearest the batteries, and another full of coal on the other, began her dash downstream. With all lights extinguished, the sky covered by an approaching thundercloud, and the engine rigged to reduce the sound of its escaping steam, all went well until sheets of flame suddenly shot out of both smoke-stacks. The gunboat, her pilots navigating only with the aid of lightning from the violent storm, at once went to full revolutions and, despite heavy bombardment from the shore, reached New Madrid in safety at 1 a.m. Two nights later she was joined by her sister-ship, *Pittsburg*, and the outnumbered Confederates surrendered on 8 April 1862.

THE ASCENT FROM NEW ORLEANS: APRIL – MAY 1862

Far away at the mouth of the river, the Navy launched its attack on New Orleans. On 18 April Porter's flotilla of twenty-one schooners, each carrying a 13in mortar, began the bombardment of the supposedly impregnable Forts Jackson and St Philip, forty miles up-river from the sea. After six days, as the forts were still holding out, Farragut ran past them with *Hartford*, four other major warships and twelve seagoing gunboats. Above the forts, he was met by eleven steamers of the Confederate River Defense Fleet. Attacking as single-tons rather than in formation, they were driven off with nine of their number sunk. A fireboat reached *Hartford*, but, after a struggle, was pushed clear. CSS *Manassas* rammed the steam-sloop *Brooklyn*, but then ran aground, caught fire, and was destroyed. CSS *Louisiana*, of which so much had been expected, was still without her engines, but had been converted to a floating battery. Set ablaze by her own crew to prevent her capture, she burnt through her mooring lines and drifted downstream to blow up near Porter's flagship *Harriet Lane*. The explosion was so violent that he and the Confederate officers with whom he was negotiating the surrender of the forts were hurled out of their chairs. *Louisiana*'s uncompleted consort *Mississippi* was burnt at her moorings.

On 26 April Farragut anchored off the New Orleans river-front, seventy-five miles above the forts, having lost one gunboat sunk and two badly damaged along the way, with 36 men killed and 135 wounded. The city that had defied the Royal Navy and Wellington's Peninsular veterans in the War of 1812 fell without further resistance. The commander of the Confederate forces in Louisiana and Texas was Major General Mansfield Lovell, born in Washington in 1822, a veteran of the Mexican War, a former cadet of the USMA, West Point and, until the outbreak of the Civil War, a first lieutenant in the United States Artillery. Most of his troops had previously been sent to join General Albert Johnston at Corinth before the battle of Shiloh, so that he had barely 3,000 men at New Orleans. Unable to defend the city, he abandoned it to Farragut, who took control pending the arrival of the Union land forces from New England under General Benjamin Butler on 1 May. Porter, irritated that Farragut had left him and the mortar-schooners behind, accepted the surrender of the forts two days later.

Farragut pressed on up the river with 1,400 soldiers, all that Butler felt able to give him, packed into two transports. Their commander, Brigadier General Thomas Williams, had served as a trumpeter in a volunteer regiment during the Black Hawk War before becoming a cadet at the USMA, West Point and joining the United States Artillery. A veteran of the Seminole and Mexican Wars, he had held various command and staff appointments in the Civil War before taking command of the 2nd Brigade in the New Orleans Expeditionary Corps. A stern disciplinarian, he declined to relax his Regular Army standards and was unpopular with his volunteer soldiers.

The gunboat (technically a 3rd-rate 6-gun steam-sloop) USS *Iroquois*, steaming ahead of the main squadron, reached Baton Rouge, the State capital of Louisiana, on 9 May and pushed on to Natchez on 12 May. Neither of these cities were defended, and their respective mayors, reluctantly giving way to *force majeure*, accepted the same terms as those offered to New Orleans. Confederate and State flags were to be replaced by that of the United States, public property was deemed contraband of war, but private property was safeguarded and the local civic authorities would be left in place. On 18 May Commander S. Phillips Lee of USS *Oneida* reached the approaches of Vicksburg, and together with Williams, sent a note to 'The Authorities of Vicksburg' stating that 'the undersigned, with orders from Flag-Officer Farragut and Major General Butler respectively, demand the surrender of Vicksburg and its defences to the lawful authority of the United States, under which private property and personal rights will be respected'.

News of the fall of New Orleans had initially caused alarm in Vicksburg. As refugees arrived from downstream, the more prudent citizens sent their families to houses outside the city. Factory owners dismantled their machinery ready for removal along the railway, and cotton owners hauled the contents of their warehouses away to be burnt rather than fall into enemy hands. The realities of war had already come to Vicksburg with the wounded of Shiloh, brought south by the trainload, and now overflowing from the city's hospitals into private households. Morale steadied when it became clear that Lovell planned to defend the city. Even before Farragut left New Orleans, its former Confederate garrison, including gunners from Forts Jackson and St Philip, had begun to move towards Vicksburg. Six regiments of Louisiana infantry, totalling 3,600 bayonets, were encamped outside the town, a brigade of Mississippi infantry was on its way to join them, and all male citizens between the ages of 18 and 50 were called upon to volunteer for local militia service.

Vicksburg, secure behind its batteries, therefore replied to Lee and Williams with defiance. Mayor Laz Lindsay, for the civil authorities, stated that they themselves had erected no defences, nor were there any within the city limits, but that nevertheless 'neither the municipal authorities nor the citizens will ever consent to the surrender of the city'. The reply from Colonel James L. Antry, the Military Governor and post commander at Vicksburg, was equally uncompromising. 'I have to state that Mississipians don't know, and refuse to learn, how to surrender to an enemy. If Commodore Farragut or Brigadier General Butler can teach them, let them come and try. As to the defences of Vicksburg, I respectfully refer you to Brigadier General Smith, commanding forces at or near Vicksburg, whose reply is herewith enclosed.' Martin L. Smith, after acknowledging receipt of the Union officers' note, simply replied 'Regarding the surrender of the defences, I have to reply that, having been ordered here to hold these defences, it is my intention to do so as long as in my power.'

The first shot was fired at 5 p.m. on 20 May 1862, when *Oneida* threw a shell at an infantry column spotted on one of the outlying bluffs. The next day Lee wrote to

Mayor Lindsay to say that it was his intention to bombard the defences and, as this would inevitably involve collateral damage in the city, he would give him twenty-four hours' notice to allow the evacuation of women and children. 'I had hoped', he added, 'that the same spirit which induced the military authorities to retire from the city of New Orleans, rather than wantonly sacrifice the lives and property of its inhabitants, would have been followed here.' Farragut arrived shortly afterwards with *Hartford*, *Brooklyn* and *Richmond*. On 26 and 27 May he exchanged shots with the batteries, but the defenders of Vicksburg, reinforced by the arrival of another Louisiana brigade with cavalry and field artillery, were unimpressed. Some citizens decided to leave by whatever means of transport had not been seized by the military, but most found shelter in cellars and prepared to take whatever the enemy could throw at them.

With Vicksburg defiant, Farragut's position became untenable. Even under the ships' guns, Williams' 1,400 men could not storm ashore against fully-manned defence works. As the Mississippi began to fall to its summer level, the levees which in winter served to keep it within its banks became natural breastworks, from which Confederate snipers could fire down onto passing vessels. The batteries high up on the bluffs became even more difficult for the guns of the warships to reach. A resurgence of Confederate activity lower down the river meant that the safe arrival of auxiliary vessels carrying fuel, ammunition and food could not be relied on. After another eight days of watching the city, Farragut took his big ships and the troops back to New Orleans, leaving a detachment of six gunboats under Commander James S. Palmer. After his departure, the gunboats *Wissahickon* and *Itasca* investigated reports of a new Confederate battery at Grand Gulf, some thirty-five miles below Vicksburg at the confluence of the Mississippi and Big Black Rivers. Unlike the turtle-shaped river gunboats, these were seagoing vessels, whose high wooden sides made them easy for the shore batteries to hit, and they were hulled forty-two times in a single short action.

THE BATTLES OF FORT PILLOW AND MEMPHIS: MAY – JUNE 1862

Meanwhile, the river flotilla continued to fight its way downstream towards Vicksburg. Most of the Confederate River Defense Fleet was destroyed in the action at New Orleans, but the survivors had gone upriver to join their consorts. On 10 May, eleven days before Farragut first reached Vicksburg, Commodore James Montgomery led thirteen gunboats and steam rams out from Fort Pillow to challenge Commodore Charles H. Davis, who had just assumed command of the Union flotilla. The lightly protected Confederate rams proved faster than the Union gunboats and struck home on *Cincinnati* and *Mound City*, both of which sank in shallow water. After four Confederate vessels had been disabled by gunfire from *Carondelet*, the rest withdrew, with their damaged consorts drifting downstream to join them under the guns of the fort. Soon afterwards they returned to a hero's welcome in Memphis. Fort Pillow was subsequently abandoned and its garrison was ordered to join the Confederate troops concentrating at Corinth.

At dawn on 6 June Davis, with his flag in *Benton*, followed by *Louisville*, *Carondelet*, *Cairo* and *St Louis*, dropped down to Memphis. *Pittsburg* and *Mound City* (salvaged and repaired along with *Cincinnati*) were left behind to protect Fort Pillow. While the gunboats exchanged fire, two of the new Ellet rams, *Queen of the West* and *Monarch*, ran past the Navy's slower vessels to attack the Confederate flotilla, which by this time had been reduced to eight gunboats and rams. *Queen of the West* struck and sank the ram *General Lovell* but was herself struck and disabled by another Confederate ram. This vessel was in turn rammed and sunk by *Monarch*, which went on to ram the Confederate gunboat *Beauregard*. *Beauregard* was then hit in the boiler by a Union shell and blew up. Of the other Confederate boats, *General Price* collided with a Confederate ram and sank after reaching the Arkansas shore; Montgomery's flagship *Little Rebel*, after being hit by gunfire, was pushed into the bank by the Union ram *Switzerland* and was abandoned, and *Jeff Thompson* ran ashore after being set on fire, and then blew up. *Sumter* and *Fort Bragg* were captured and, of the eight Confederate boats in the battle, only *Van Dorn*, using her superior speed to escape down-river, survived. The entire action, involving the expenditure of some 300 rounds of heavy ammunition by the Union vessels, lasted less than an hour. The inhabitants of Memphis, watching the fight from the bluffs above their city, with many of the ladies reduced to tears as each of their boats were lost, were left with no choice but surrender. On the Union side, Colonel Charles Ellet, Jr, originator of the Union ram fleet, was the only significant casualty. Seriously wounded, he died two weeks later and his place was taken by his brother, Alfred W. Ellet, who became brigadier general commanding the Mississippi Marine Brigade.

THE NAVAL ATTACK: JUNE – JULY 1862

With the way down to Vicksburg clear, Farragut was sent back upstream under orders from Lincoln himself, to use his utmost exertions 'to open the Mississippi and make a junction with Flag-Officer Davis'. This time, he would take Porter with him, to use the mortars' high trajectory against the positions on Vicksburg's bluffs. Williams, his bayonet strength increased to 3,000, would accompany them. Re-assembling with some difficulty his fleet train of coal barges and supply boats, Farragut moved back up the river with sixteen mortar-schooners under tow, picked up his detached gunboats and reached Vicksburg on 25 June. Williams disembarked his men from their passenger steamers and established a position on the De Soto Peninsula.

On 27 June the mortar-schooners, moored on both sides of the river, their high masts camouflaged by branches, fired their first ranging shots. At 2 a.m. next morning the squadron got under way in two lines. The three full-rigged ships, with *Richmond* leading, Farragut in his flagship *Hartford* in the centre and *Brooklyn* bringing up the rear, formed one line. The gunboats *Iroquois, Wissahickon, Scioto, Winona, Pinola, Kennebec* and *Katahdin*, led by Commander S. Phillips Lee in *Oneida*, formed another, parallel to it, spaced so that they could fire through the intervals between the big ships. In support, Porter came up with the armed paddle-steamers *Clifton, Jackson, Harriet Lane* and *Oswego* from his mortar flotilla. At 4 a.m. the mortars began to shoot over the squadron to engage the batteries above the city.

In reply, Vicksburg opened fire on the approaching warships, with heavy guns in the waterside batteries and on the bluffs, field guns pointing down the streets of the city and infantry firing either in regular volleys or as individual sharpshooters. Farragut's big ships replied with their broadsides and the gunboats with their single 11-in smooth-bores and Parrott guns. From the Louisiana bank, Williams' field pieces joined in, hoping to distract the Confederate gunners. *Hartford* steamed ahead at a slow speed, at one time stopping to allow *Brooklyn* and the rest of the squadron to close up. The deceptive light of dawn and river-mist was soon succeeded by a literal fog of war, as steam and coal-smoke from the ships mingled with the smoke of their guns and that of the shore batteries. At one point the gunners, firing respectively at or from moving targets, were reduced to aiming at the flash of one another's discharges.

The poor visibility and bad shooting by the Confederate batteries allowed *Hartford* to pass the city virtually unscathed, though the guns on the upstream side made better practice. *Oneida* was hit four times, but fired a total of seventy-eight rounds from her various guns, while the gunboat *Pinola*, the last vessel to pass the batteries, fired eighty-six rounds and was hit seven times. All told, the squadron lost seventeen killed and thirty wounded, including six scalded to death and others injured by escaping steam when *Clifton*, going to the help of the disabled *Jackson*, was hit in a boiler by a 7-in shell and was in turn disabled.

When the smoke cleared after the bulk of the squadron had passed the batteries, Captain Craven of *Brooklyn* found himself alone with *Kennebec* and *Katahdin*. The mortar-schooners had been taken back downstream to the shelter of the woods along the bank. Of the flag and the rest of the squadron there was no sign. As Farragut's orders were that the big ships, together with *Iroquois* and *Oneida* should not pass Vicksburg leaving any batteries unsilenced behind them, and as most of the Confederate gun positions were still in action after an engagement lasting two hours and forty minutes, Craven stopped his engines and went down the river to anchor about two and a half miles below Vicksburg. Above the city, Farragut made contact with Alfred W. Ellet's rams and waited for Davis, who joined him on 1 July with four gunboats and five mortar-boats.

Porter, in his report to Farragut, summed up the problem. 'Ships and mortar-vessels can keep full possession of the river and places near the water's edge, but they cannot crawl up hills three hundred feet high, and it is that part of Vicksburg which must be taken by the army. If it was intended merely to pass the batteries at Vicksburg and make a junction with the fleet of Flag-Officer Davis, the Navy did it most gallantly and fearlessly.' He was critical of the army for not making a combined attack, which he believed would have carried the town. Williams, however, was still on the Louisiana side of the river. An attempt at an opposed landing, even with the close support of the squadron, would have been suicidal, and with only 3,000 men at his disposal against a Confederate garrison reported to be 17,000 strong, an attack from the landward side, after crossing somewhere downstream, would have proved equally disastrous for his troops.

Porter had to rely on his own resources to defend the mortar-schooners moored on the Vicksburg side of the river. Anticipating a threat from the shore, he set up a line of patrols in the trees and swamps along the bank, with his guns trained along likely approach routes. These precautions drove off an attack by Confederate infantry on 1 July, after which Porter landed five howitzers and a large ship's bell, with lines leading to it from the various sentry positions. After the failure of a second attack the following day, the schooners were left undisturbed apart from periodic long-range shelling by Confederate artillery. The mortars opened a steady bombardment on the defences, only to be met with continued defiance. They were in any case needed elsewhere and on 10 July Porter left with twelve of his schooners to join the fleet at Norfolk, Virginia.

THE ARKANSAS: JUNE – AUGUST 1862

There had long been reports that a Confederate ironclad was under construction somewhere up the Yazoo. On 26 June, as Farragut prepared to run the batteries at Vicksburg, Colonel Alfred W. Ellet and the teenaged Lieutenant Colonel Charles Rivers Ellet (a former medical cadet and son of the late Colonel Charles Ellet, Jr) went in search of her but, after fifty miles, found only two gunboats and a ram, which were set on fire by their crews to avoid capture. What they were looking for was the CSS *Arkansas*, laid down at Memphis but taken two hundred miles up the Yazoo to the head of navigation at Greenwood, Mississippi, to avoid Davis' approaching flotilla. There, her new commander, Lieutenant Isaac N. Brown, found her partly submerged in the flooded river, four miles from hard ground, without power, gun-carriages or armour. With remarkable inventiveness and energy, he took her downstream to Yazoo City, where he scavenged men, materials and machinery, mounted the guns, fitted the armour and restored the low-pressure engines that drove her twin screws. When ready for service, she measured 165 feet overall, and carried eight guns, ranging from 6-in rifled cannon to 64-pdr smooth-bores. On 12 July *Arkansas*, with a 200-strong crew made up partly of sailors from the boats destroyed on the approach of the Ellets and partly of army volunteers to whom maritime warfare was completely new, moved under her own steam to Satartia, fifty miles up the Yazoo from the Mississippi confluence.

On 15 July Farragut sent *Carondelet*, *Taylor* and *Queen of the West* into the Yazoo to look for her. Soon after entering the river they met her coming down. The Union boats rapidly reversed course, firing at *Arkansas* to little effect, while the shots from her heavy guns repeatedly pierced *Carondelet*'s iron sides. Commander Walke of *Carondelet*, who had served with Brown in the US Navy before the war, found his steering shot away and was left with his boat listing and aground, in a cloud of smoke and escaping steam. Although the sound of gunfire could be heard where Farragut and Davis lay at anchor, it was not until *Taylor* and *Queen of the West* appeared at full speed from the mouth of the Yazoo, closely pursued by *Arkansas*, that the nature of the action was appreciated. Not a single Union vessel there was in steam, nor was there time for those that had sails even to think of using them.

Arkansas dashed through them, exchanging broadsides on the way, and reached the protection of the Vicksburg batteries amid the rejoicing of its garrison and citizens. On the way, she had passed some twenty Union war vessels, damaging *Hartford*, *Iroquois* and *Benton*, disabling the ram *Lancaster* with a shot through the steam drum, and inflicting total casualties of eighteen killed and sixty wounded or missing, half as many as Farragut had lost in the approach to New Orleans. In the process, *Arkansas* had sustained almost the same number of casualties among her own crew, most of whom were volunteers engaged only for the single run to Vicksburg. Moreover, she had suffered considerable damage, not least to her temperamental engines. Coming alongside the Vicksburg waterfront, Brown landed his dead and wounded as the cheers of the shocked spectators died away, refilled his empty bunkers and began repairs.

Farragut decided to take his squadron downstream at dusk to sink *Arkansas* at her moorings, while the river gunboats *Benton*, *Cincinnati* and *Louisville* engaged the upper batteries. Lying under the shadow of the bank, the ram was an impossible target for the Union gunners to make out. She attempted to get under way with the intention of ramming one of the passing warships, but was stopped when a shot from *Oneida* penetrated her engine-room. Exchanging fire with the waterside batteries, *Hartford* was hulled several times. *Iroquois*' engines suddenly stopped and she drifted downstream for twenty minutes until the chief engineer got them restarted. *Richmond* received ten hits. *Winona*, hit on the water-line, found the water gaining on her pumps and after almost reaching the designated anchorage site below Vicksburg, was run aground in eleven feet of water, with one man killed and two wounded.

On 22 July Farragut, having re-united his squadron, ordered Davis' mortar-boats to open fire while *Essex*, under Captain William 'Dirty Bill' Porter (elder brother of David D. Porter), and *Queen of the West* ran down at full speed to sink *Arkansas* at her moorings. At the critical moment, *Arkansas* (moored like all river-boats, to face upstream) let go her forward line, so that her bow was swung out by the current to lie at right angles to the bank. *Essex*, unable to alter her angle of attack, ran into the bank where *Arkansas* had been lying and stuck fast. The two vessels, now alongside each other, exchanged fire at point-blank range, but neither side inflicted serious damage. Only three shots pierced *Essex*'s armour and after about ten minutes she was backed off and went downstream to join Farragut, having lost one man killed and three wounded. Meanwhile *Queen of the West* had been so heavily damaged by gunfire that she was unable to begin her ramming run and was forced to return upstream. *Arkansas* still remained a potent threat, and by keeping up steam day and night, so as to give the appearance of being ready to come out, obliged the entire Union fleet to do likewise, draining their coal and exhausting their stokers in the fierce heat of the Mississippi summer. Vicksburg, having withstood four weeks' continuous bombardment, was more defiant than ever.

Ashore, Williams decided that he could no longer hold his position. As agreed with Farragut, his troops, with a labour force of some 1,500 African-Americans liberated from neighbouring plantations, had dug a narrow canal across the neck of the De Soto Peninsula. By mid-July a cut eighteen feet wide and thirteen feet deep had been made, but the steadily falling level of the water meant that it was never navigable and served only as a defence line against the threat of a raid from Vicksburg. Williams was defeated, in the event, not by Southern soldiers, but by Southern mosquitoes. The same swampy ground that protected the moored mortar-schooners and allowed the construction of canals and ditches also provided breeding-grounds for the carriers of malaria or 'swamp fever'. At the time, however, few associated the fevers with the mosquitoes, and blame was generally placed on the 'miasma' or unhealthy vapour from the evaporation of stagnant water. In New Orleans and other southern cities, reliance was placed on burning tar barrels and the discharge of cannon to disperse the bad air (the *mal-aria*). The day after the failure of the second attempt to sink *Arkansas*, Farragut reported to the Secretary of the Navy that Williams was preparing to leave Vicksburg because he 'had not well men enough to take care of the sick ones'. With the river falling to its late summer levels and placing the seagoing ships at risk from grounding, Farragut took his squadron and the soldiers downstream on 24 July 1862.

Above the city, Davis found his own position untenable. Union logistic vessels could no longer be moored safely along the bank, he had lost touch with *Essex*, five of his remaining gunboats were under repair and another three were guarding vital points up-stream, while the unarmed transports were constantly shot at by Confederate marksmen and horse artillery. Moreover, the disease that had laid low so many of Williams' soldiers had also struck Davis' sailors. Of the hundred and thirty men on the establishment of his mortar-boats, only thirty were fit for duty, and he needed another five or six hundred men to replace casualties among the rest of the flotilla. 'The most sickly part of the season is approaching and the Department would be surprised to see how the most healthy men wilt and break down under the ceaseless and exhausting heat of this pernicious climate. Men who are apparently in health at the close of the day's work, sink away and die suddenly at night, under the combined effect of heat and malarial poison', he wrote in his own report to the Secretary of the Navy. He left Vicksburg at the same time as Farragut and on 31 July anchored at Helena, Arkansas, two hundred miles upstream.

Downstream, Williams landed his troops at Baton Rouge, where he remained as unpopular as ever, not least when he arrested several officers for failing to return a number of runaway slaves. In return, charges were brought against him, but these were still unresolved when he was attacked on 4 August by a Confederate force under Major General John C. Breckinridge. The attack was beaten off, with the support of fire from the gunboats *Essex*, *Katahdin* and *Kineo*, directed by one of *Kineo*'s officers from the tower of Baton Rouge State House. Williams himself was killed in the fighting, with a rumour that he was shot by his own men.

The Confederates had counted upon *Arkansas* to arrive from Vicksburg to deal with the gunboats and, at the beginning of the action, both sides saw the smoke as she approached the bend above Baton Rouge. Suddenly she stopped, her port engine having broken down, and she spent the next two days undergoing repairs. On the morning of 7 August, *Essex* went upstream from Baton Rouge to seek out her old adversary. *Arkansas* came down to meet her, but her starboard engine then broke down, and, under fire from *Essex*, she was run ashore and set on fire by her crew. She then drifted back into the river, where she blew up and sank. Brown, who had been ashore sick when his command was ordered to sail, caught up with her only in time to see her go down. Breckinridge marched twenty-five miles northwards from Baton Rouge to Port Hudson, where he established what would become the strongest Confederate position on the river after Vicksburg itself. The Mississippi remained closed to Northern traffic and the flow of food, men, and raw materials from Texas and Louisiana to the Confederate heartland continued as before.

GRANT'S OPERATIONS IN NORTHERN MISSISSIPPI: DECEMBER 1862 – JANUARY 1863

Elsewhere, the war was going equally badly for the Union. The mid-term elections were approaching and many voters in the North began to question whether the preservation of the Union really justified the cost in lives of the nation's young men and the disruption of the national economy. Lincoln issued the Edict of Emancipation, declaring that slaves in those states in rebellion against the USA would become free on 1 January 1863. This gave much moral impetus to the Union cause, but however much abolitionists might rejoice, and irrespective of the delight of slaves of Southern plantations at the sight of what the minstrel groups called 'de smoke, way up de ribber, where de Linkum gunboats lay', the Mid-West still saw the river-road blocked against its commerce.

Lincoln therefore determined that another effort must be made against Vicksburg, this time with the Army as the main force of the attack. The need to send reinforcements to counter a Confederate thrust from eastern Tennessee at first obliged Grant to stand on the defensive, but in a skilfully handled engagement at Iuka on 19 September he forced the Confederates to retreat. They regrouped and made a determined attack on Corinth, but were once again defeated on 3–4

October. At the end of the month, Grant was formally appointed to command what would become the Army of the Tennessee, with the capture of Vicksburg as his prime objective.

Grant's first plan was to move westwards from Corinth with 30,000 men and follow the line of the Mississippi Central Railroad southwards for 200 miles through Holly Springs, Oxford and Granada to Jackson. From there, Vicksburg was only forty or so miles to the west. He appreciated that his Confederate opponent, Lieutenant General John C. Pemberton, had a similar number of men, but, having won a series of hard-fought victories, was confident that his own troops were a match for them. His main anxiety at this time lay in the organisation of his own side and, in particular, in the ambitions of his subordinate, Major General John A. McClernand. McClernand had recently been to Washington and persuaded his old friend Lincoln to send him to the Mid-Western States to boost their flagging support for the war and repeat his recruiting successes of the previous year.

Porter, newly promoted to acting rear-admiral, was in Washington at the same time, on the way to succeed Davis in command of the Upper Mississippi flotilla. He waited upon Lincoln and, when asked for his opinion on the best general to take Vicksburg, replied that Grant was best placed for the overall command, and would probably send Sherman, of whom Porter thought highly. He was astonished to find that Lincoln had decided to give command of the operation to McClernand, who, in the President's view, had won the victory at Shiloh. Porter expressed his doubts, but Lincoln would not be moved and instructed him to call on McClernand. Hurrying to join his command at Cairo, Porter sent a note to Gustavus Fox, Assistant Secretary of the Navy, outlining McClernand's plans. Commenting that McClernand was soon to be married, he added, with a sailor's salty humour, 'if he proposes to recruit an army in that way, I think it will hardly be worth while to wait for him'.

Lincoln's orders to McClernand, when finally drawn up by Halleck, authorised him to raise his new Mid-Western troops, but went on to add, somewhat obscurely, that 'when a sufficient force, not required by the operations of General Grant's command shall be raised, an expedition may be organised under General McClernand's command against Vicksburg'. On 10 November, marching on Holly Springs, Grant read newspaper stories that McClernand was to operate as an independent commander. In the laconic prose style that does credit to his West Point education, Grant afterwards wrote in his Memoirs: 'Two commanders in the same field are always one too many, and in this case I did not think that the general selected had either the experience or qualifications to fit him for so important a position.' He asked Halleck (who shared Grant's view of McClernand's military abilities) what was going on and was told 'You have command of all the troops sent to your department and have permission to fight the enemy where you please.'

Nevertheless, Grant had every reason to press on before McClernand reasserted his political influence, which would become all the stronger if he raised enough recruits to justify an independent command. He accordingly pushed south to reach Oxford, Mississippi, by 8 December. From there he sent Sherman back to Memphis with an experienced division, wanting to have someone competent in charge of McClernand's new regiments when they arrived there. While Grant continued his operations in the interior, Sherman was to take command at Memphis and move the combined force down the Mississippi to attack Vicksburg from the Yazoo.

This plan was disrupted when Major General Earl Van Dorn and 3,500 Confederate horsemen attacked Grant's supply depot at Holly Springs at dawn on 20 December. Most of the 1,500-strong Union garrison was captured and the stores on which Grant was relying were put to the torch. His wife, Mrs Julia Dent Grant, only narrowly escaped this débâcle, having left for Oxford the previous day. At the same time, Nathan Bedford Forrest, one of the Confederacy's boldest cavalry commanders, conducted a series of raids behind Grant's lines, cutting railroads and telegraph wires. With his logistic base destroyed and his supply line vulnerable to raiders, Grant decided to abandon his offensive. As no more provisions to feed his hungry men and horses would be coming down the battered railway, he sent out foraging parties to commandeer whatever could be found. They were amazed to discover what this fertile and prosperous country had in its barns and storehouses. It would be possible, Grant noted, for an army to live off the land, not merely for the two weeks that it would take to rejoin his base, but for two months. Local citizens who had gleefully supposed that Grant's men would starve now faced the same prospect themselves and were advised by him to travel fifteen miles southwards, where they could be fed by their friends.

In the cold and wet weather of northern Mississippi's mid-winter, he began his retreat from Oxford on 21 December. He found his march hampered not only by the poor roads but by thousands of slaves, men, women and children, whose masters had fled before Grant's advance. Not freedmen until 1 January 1863, they were still technically 'contraband' and as such the responsibility of the Union commanders to whom they fled. Fit young men could be employed by the army as pioneers, wagon-drivers or cooks, but providing for the remainder posed a problem until Grant eventually used them to pick cotton (also classified as contraband) from abandoned plantations. During his retreat, with nowhere else to go, and fearing to fall into the hands of Forrest (after the war he founded and became Grand Wizard of the Ku Klux Klan) they went with him, many clinging desperately to the sides and roofs of overloaded rolling stock on the line back to Memphis.

SHERMAN'S ATTACK ON THE CHICKASAW BLUFFS (THE WALNUT HILLS): DECEMBER 1862

Meanwhile, Porter's flotilla, reinforced by the arrival of the shallow-draught lightly armoured 'tinclads', began a reconnaissance of the Yazoo. On 11 December the light gunboats *Marmora* and *Signal* went about sixteen miles up the river without opposition from the various bluffs that lined the southern bank. They then found the river blocked by submarine mines ('torpedoes' in the terminology of the day), buoyed up by a collection of rafts and small craft. Two days later they returned, accompanied by the ironclads *Cairo* and *Pittsburg* and the ram *Queen of the West*. The plan was for *Marmora* and *Signal* to clear the mines by sending parties ahead to haul them ashore, covered by the naval artillery on the gunboats and by the marines firing from *Queen of the West*'s high decks. When *Marmora*'s crew decided to explode the floating mines by shooting at them with musketry, *Cairo* came forward expecting to join in an action, but hit two mines and immediately began to take in water. She reached the bank, only a few yards away, but with the water gaining rapidly on the pumps, her captain had barely time to remove his sick and the gunboat's small arms. After twelve minutes she slid into deep water and sank in six fathoms, the first vessel in naval history to be lost to a mine, while her crew was rescued by *Queen of the West*.

Sherman reached Memphis on 12 December and began his move down the river on the 20th. Quite apart from his own inclination to press on with the operation, he was under pressure to leave before McClernand arrived to succeed him. Grant himself later wrote in his Memoirs that he had timed Sherman's

Chickasaw Bluffs. Running north-east from Vicksburg, the Walnut Hills formed a perfect fortress, rising to some 200 feet. In the 12 miles between Haynes' Bluff and the city, there were only a few places where troops could pass from the Yazoo through the bayous and swamps to reach the bluffs.

departure to forestall McClernand and that he had good reason to believe that this had the tacit approval of his superiors. Sherman sailed on the day before Grant turned back from Oxford on 21 December but, because Confederate raiders had cut the telegraph wires, none of Grant's messages reached Memphis in time to recall Sherman from what was his first major independent operation. Under the impression that Grant was still marching towards Jackson and thereby occupying the bulk of the Confederate forces in the area, Sherman took his army up the Yazoo and on 26 December began to disembark on the southern bank, heading for the Chickasaw Bluffs.

There were only a few landing-stages, designed to serve the needs of local plantations, and it was not until sunset on the following day that all the troops were ashore. The first division to arrive advanced towards Vicksburg along the levees and country roads, exchanging shots with Confederate skirmishers. The rain-soaked low-lying country slowed movement, and progress towards the Confederate-held Haynes' and Snyder's Bluffs was made more difficult by a series of deep muddy bayous. As soon as Pemberton learned of Sherman's landings, he moved troops south along the railway from Grenada and thence to Vicksburg. By sunset on 27 December, three brigades had arrived, effectively doubling the size of the garrison, while the recently promoted Major General Martin L. Smith lined the bluffs with guns and men from the city.

With the aim of clearing a place where Sherman could land troops between the bluffs and the area nearer the city, so splitting the Confederate forces, the gunboats returned to mine-clearing duties. With their shallow draught, all the river-boats were difficult to handle in the gale then blowing, and *Benton*, leading the way, was so prone to turn broadside into the wind that she had to be tied up alongside the bank, thereby becoming a stationary target for an eight-gun shore battery. After two hours, in which she received thirty hits and suffered ten casualties among her crew (her commanding officer and executive officer both being seriously wounded) the action was called off and *Benton* rejoined her consorts.

During 28 December Sherman's troops, their progress impeded by various natural and man-made obstacles, reached the forward edge of the Confederate line. Next morning, still unaware of Grant's retreat, he launched an attack up through the swamps and broken ground in an attempt to carry the heights. This was met by a storm of artillery and musketry fire. After losing 208 killed and 1,005 wounded, against Confederate losses of 63 and 134 respectively, his men could do no more. They fell back on their start-line and bivouacked on the water-logged ground with nothing to shelter them from the rain but their blankets, while their generals exchanged accusations of cowardice, incompetence or rashness. Aboard his flagship, Porter did his best to cheer the dejected mud-soaked Sherman and, while the Confederates constructed further defences, devised a new plan, for a night attack on Drumgould's Bluff, further up the Yazoo. This scheme was frustrated when a dense mist sprang up, reducing visibility to ten yards. With the boats unable to see each other or the channel, and every sign of the mist being succeeded by a further spell of heavy rain, the expedition was cancelled.

On the morning of 2 January 1863 the whole of Sherman's army had re-embarked before the Confederates discovered what was happening. Field guns hastily sent to bombard the departing transports were silenced by the gunboats and in the afternoon the entire flotilla steamed out of the Yazoo and headed upstream to disembark in pouring rain at Milliken's Bend, on the Louisiana bank some twenty miles above Vicksburg. Notwithstanding the achievement of the Union forces in embarking an army without loss in the presence of an enemy, one of the most hazardous operations of war, they had suffered a clear defeat. Vicksburg had beaten off a third attack and the Confederate flag still proudly waved over the city that Jefferson Davis called 'the nail-head that held the two halves of the Confederacy together'. Sherman, in one of the shortest post-operational reports after Julius Caesar's *Veni, vidi, vici*, wrote 'I reached Vicksburg at the time appointed, landed, assaulted and failed, re-embarked my command and turned it over to my successor.'

McClernand had spent much of December awaiting orders to join his troops at Memphis. Halleck now told him that, although he was still the designated commander of the Mississippi operation, his army would not be an independent command, but a corps in Grant's Army of the Tennessee. Grant telegraphed McClernand with the requisite orders to take command at Memphis, but, because the wires had been cut by Confederate raiders, these were no more successfully delivered than his earlier messages notifying Sherman of the retreat from Oxford. It was not until 23 December that McClernand received his joining orders via the Army Department in Washington. Consoled only by the charms of his new bride (the 26-year-old Minerva Dunlap, his deceased wife's sister), he arrived at Memphis on 28 December to find that his troops had already gone to Vicksburg. After they disembarked at Milliken's Bend, he at last took over their command from Sherman. McClernand began by naming his force 'The Army of the Mississippi' and dividing it into two corps, with Sherman in command of one of them. He then agreed to Sherman's proposal for a raid into Arkansas, to secure the Mississippi between Memphis and Vicksburg against any Confederate attack from the west. Porter had taken a dislike to McClernand, but was persuaded by Sherman to accompany them.

THE CAPTURE OF FORT HINDMAN (THE ARKANSAS POST): JANUARY 1863

Grant told McClernand that it would be 'a wild goose chase', though he subsequently gave it his approval when he discovered that Sherman had suggested it. A strong force accordingly steamed the hundred and fifty miles upstream to enter the Arkansas River, and thence to Fort Hindman. This, also known as the Arkansas Post, was a well-fortified position some forty miles up the river from the Mississippi confluence and a hundred below Little Rock, the Arkansas State capital. On 9 January 1863 the troops landed about four miles below this position and marched inland to attack from the landward side. Meanwhile the gunboats pushed on, and in the late afternoon the ironclads *Louisville*, *De Kalb* and *Cincinnati* closed to within 500 yards of the defence works and opened fire. Their consorts, *Lexington*, *Black Hawk* (Porter's flagship) and the shallow-draught tinclads *Glide*, *New Era*, *Signal*, *Rattler* and *Romeo*, moved up under cover of the smoke and joined in the attack. A Confederate steamer, CSS *Cotton*, was driven back and sank after being set on fire.

On the landward side the army halted at the edge of the Confederate lines and during the night Sherman personally crept to within earshot of the defences. With the dawn his troops advanced to contact, facing a spirited resistance while the gunboats resumed their bombardment and *Monarch* ran past to cut off the garrison's line of retreat. During the fighting the Confederates lost 60 killed and 80 wounded against McClernand's 134 killed, 898 wounded and 29 missing, with thirty casualties among the flotilla. Heavily outnumbered and with his defences shattered by the fire of the gunboats, the Confederate commander, Brigadier General Thomas J. Churchill, a Kentucky lawyer turned Arkansas planter, was forced to surrender with nearly 5,000 men, seventeen guns and 563 draught animals.

From his headquarters in the steamboat *Tigress*, McClernand wrote a report describing his victory in glowing terms, speaking highly of Sherman's performance under his command, but paying scant regard to the part played by Porter, to whom alone Colonel Dunnington, commanding the water-side defences, had insisted on giving up his sword. Both Sherman and Porter wrote to Grant to express their distrust of McClernand's abilities and urged him to come and take command in person. The expedition returned to the confluence of the Arkansas and Mississippi, where Grant arrived on 17 January. McClernand thought that, having achieved a significant victory with troops whom he had found doing nothing, he might have received Grant's congratulations, and wrote to Lincoln to complain of being persecuted by 'a clique of West Pointers'. Grant decided that, as he could scarcely relieve so senior and well-connected an officer from his command, nor place him under a more capable junior (Sherman), the only course open was to combine the forces in his Department into a single army, with himself in direct command. On 20 January he ordered McClernand's troops down to Young's Point, on the west bank of the Mississippi opposite the confluence with the Yazoo.

Far to the east, General Joseph E. Johnston, since November 1862 commanding the newly created Confederate Military Department of the West, decided that Major General Braxton Bragg needed reinforcements for his Army of Tennessee. With both Grant and Sherman defeated, there seemed no immediate danger to Vicksburg and he accordingly ordered Major General Earl Van Dorn to take two-thirds of Pemberton's cavalry (at that time located at Grenada), form it into a division and march with it to join Bragg. Johnston's view was that these horsemen were not actually being employed and, from the flooded state of the country, could not usefully be so until the spring.

SWAMP WARFARE

THE MOVES TO OUTFLANK VICKSBURG:
JANUARY – APRIL 1863

THE DE SOTO CANAL: JANUARY – MARCH 1863

On 30 January 1863 Grant took personal command of the troops at Young's Point and set about reorganising his forces. McClernand's Army of the Mississippi was absorbed into the Army of the Tennessee, with one of its two corps, renamed XV Corps, remaining under Sherman and the other, renamed XIII Corps, left for McClernand. Together with XVII Corps under Major General James B. McPherson upstream of Young's Point at Milliken's Bend, this gave Grant an army of 62,000 men, backed by XVI Corps under Major General Stephen A. Hurlbut holding the line from Memphis into western Tennessee. The disappointed McClernand protested in vigorous (in Grant's view, insubordinate) terms and complained indignantly to Lincoln, suggesting for good measure that Lincoln himself should take over command of the Union armies from Halleck. Lincoln, who had indeed led McClernand to believe that he would head the march on Vicksburg, soothed his old friend's injured feelings and urged him to concentrate his energies against the Confederates.

Grant appreciated that the ground on either side of the Mississippi, consisting mostly of low-lying swamps full of standing and fallen timber and intersected by a maze of bayous, would be impassable in the face of an enemy. The first course open was to return to Memphis, establish a well-defended base there, and then repeat his moves of the previous month by marching on good ground along the railway (repairing it as he went) to Jackson. This was strongly advocated by Sherman, but Grant rejected it as politically unacceptable. With the war going badly for the Union, it would look like another retreat, at a time when the mid-term elections were approaching and support for what his opponents had dubbed 'Mr Lincoln's War' seemed to be ebbing away. If he could neither go back, nor go down, he would have to go round. Immediate action was required, not least by Lincoln, who remained fascinated by the river and by Vicksburg. The troops needed active employment, for the sake of both their morale and their health. The winter rains of 1862–63 were the worst on record and the river was particularly high, with nowhere to pitch tents except on the levees that ran for mile after mile along its banks. Cold and exposure added to the inevitable diseases ('camp fever') arising from the poor sanitation of tens of thousands of men and animals. Troops accommodated on transports escaped the all-pervading mud but, crowded together, were easy prey to infections. There was even an outbreak of cholera in Grant's own headquarters ship, the steamboat *Magnolia*.

On his arrival at Young's Point, Grant found that, at Lincoln's suggestion, McClernand had already started to re-open Williams' canal across the De Soto

Peninsula. Remembering the Mississippi's tendency to cut across its meanders, Lincoln envisaged it scouring out a new channel along the canal, so opening the way to the sea and leaving Vicksburg as an irrelevant inland town. Unfortunately for this plan, there was insufficient fall between the upper and lower sides of the peninsula to draw the stream from its existing natural channel. Moreover, Williams had begun his canal where there was a back eddy. Instead of rushing downstream, the water at this point circled lazily back towards the centre of the river. Nevertheless, Grant allowed the work to go on, partly out of deference to Lincoln, whom he had every reason to conciliate, and partly to give the troops an alternative to freezing or rotting in their water-logged camps. Supported by gangs of freedmen from nearby plantations and by steam dredgers sent down the river on Lincoln's orders, they dug steadily along, their progress being observed by Confederate look-outs in Vicksburg.

THE LAKE PROVIDENCE WATERWAY: JANUARY – FEBRUARY 1863

Meanwhile, Grant ordered McPherson to begin another project. This was to open a water route from Milliken's Bend to the oxbow Lake Providence and thence through a series of bayous and navigable rivers to the Red River, flowing into the Mississippi above the Confederate batteries at Port Hudson. The difficulties of clearing a way through the bayous were even greater than those of by-passing Island No 10 the previous March. With barely two feet of water in some places, a channel had to be dredged that would take not merely the shallow-draught boats that had sufficed at New Madrid, but heavy ironclads that might be needed anywhere along the way. Where the water was deep, standing timber was cut down close to the bottom, using specially designed underwater circular saws. Everywhere, fallen or felled trees had to be dragged out of the water and hauled into barges to be towed away. Grant visited the work-site on 4 February and found that McPherson had decided not to open a cut into Lake Providence until he had cleared a way through the bayous. Nevertheless, a thirty-ton steam-boat had been hauled the short distance overland from the Mississippi and was serving as a reconnaissance and dispatch vessel. Visitors were entertained with cruises and regimental bands, and the troops enjoyed fishing in their off-duty moments. Grant, however, had calculated that the distance from Milliken's Bend to the confluence of the Mississippi and the Red River was 470 miles, even going directly downstream. The route through the backwaters and tributaries would be even longer, with Confederate opposition very likely as soon as the big rivers were reached. He therefore concluded that the Lake Providence plan was impracticable, and had already decided to try another waterway, on the east side of the river.

This was through the levee at Delta, six miles below Helena, Arkansas, and 120 above Milliken's Bend. Until six years previously, it had been an established route, the Yazoo Pass, through which steamboats could travel from the Mississippi into the Coldwater River and then down the Tallahatchie to its confluence with the Yazoo above Greenwood. This route gave direct access from Helena to Yazoo City and the upper Yazoo basin and represented significant savings in coal and time. Nevertheless, it had been shut off by the Mississippi State authorities in 1857, to protect the neighbouring plantations from flood and to allow swamp-land to be reclaimed for agriculture. On 2 February Grant's engineers blew up the levee that closed the Pass. The river, at this time nine feet higher than the surrounding countryside, poured through, filling up the old channels and flooding the country for miles around. After four days the water was level and a flotilla under Lieutenant Commander Watson Smith steamed through the broken levee. With him were the heavy ironclads *Chillicothe* (one of a new class of gunboat, driven by side-wheels placed amidships, and carrying their guns in fixed turrets) and *De Kalb*, the tug *Bayard* and the shallow-draught tinclads *Forest Rose*, *Marmora*, *Rattler*, *Romeo* and *Signal*. Following them, after some delay in embarking at Helena, were fourteen transports with 4,500 infantry under Brigadier General Leonard F. Ross. The hope was that, once they reached the Yazoo, Grant's entire army would be able to follow and then come down that river to disembark upstream of the batteries at Haynes' and Drumgould's Bluffs.

The Union 'tinclad' *Rattler*, command vessel of Lieutenant Commander Watson Smith on the Yazoo River in 1863.

THE QUEEN OF THE WEST AND THE INDIANOLA: FEBRUARY 1863

On the same day that Watson Smith entered the Yazoo Pass, Porter sent *Queen of the West*, the pride of the Ellet ram-fleet, down past Vicksburg to disrupt the Confederate traffic still running from Louisiana and Texas. Her commander, the teenaged Colonel Charles R. Ellet, steamed beyond the confluence with the Red River and returned to the lower side of the De Soto Peninsula three days later, having sunk four Confederate steamers. With enough coal to last a month, he again went down river, accompanied by *De Soto* (a captured steamboat converted to a Union cotton-clad), burning waterside plantations and flatboats as he went. On 12 February he turned into the Red River, captured the steamer *Era No 5* and pushed on to Gordon's Landing. There *Queen of the West* came under fire at 400 yards' range from the heavy shore battery, Fort De Russey. Her regular pilot, who had brought her past Vicksburg, was ill and his replacement, a Mr Garocy, when ordered to back away, promptly ran her aground on a mud-bank, where she lost all power when her steam-pipe was hit. While some of his crew escaped the scalding clouds of steam in a yawl, most jumped overboard, using the ram's protective cotton bales as life-rafts. Ellet himself, having watched his boat settle in ten feet of water, was among the last to join them. Those who delayed too long were captured by Confederate boarders, who put out from the bank in swarms of small boats. The survivors were picked up by *De Soto*, which then ran downstream. When a thick river-mist sprang up, she collided with the bank and lost her rudder, but was able to drift with the current for fifteen miles until she rejoined the unarmed *Era No 5*. Ellet then scuttled and burnt *De Soto* and made for the Mississippi in *Era No 5* through a night of thunderstorms and continued mist. To increase speed and decrease draught he threw her valuable cargo over the side, knowing that somewhere behind was the Confederate ram *William H. Webb*, a converted tow-boat capable of making fourteen knots, against which Porter had particularly warned him. On reaching the Mississippi, the pilot Garocy again ran his vessel aground and this time allowed the paddle wheels to continue turning forward after she had stopped. Reporting that Garocy had only a few hours earlier expressed 'disloyal sentiments', Ellet placed him under arrest, got *Era No 5* off after passing the night a few yards away from the Confederate-held bank and headed upstream on the morning of 13 February, making a single knot against the fast-running current.

Unaware of these events, Porter sent another boat past Vicksburg during the night of 13 February, to join Ellet in his commerce-raiding operations. This was *Indianola*, the newest and largest ironclad in the flotilla, armed forward and aft with 11-in and 9-in guns and propelled both by paddle-wheels and screws. After meeting *Era No 5* at dawn on 14 February, her commanding officer, Lieutenant Commander George Brown, took the two boats downstream and sighted *William*

H. Webb, which immediately went back into the Red River. The Union boats reached the confluence on 17 February, after which *Era No 5* was sent to the anchorage below Vicksburg. *Indianola*, unable to find a Red River pilot, remained in position until 21 February 1863, when Brown learnt that *Queen of the West* had been raised and repaired and, together with *William H. Webb* and four cotton-clads (in fact only two came out) was preparing for battle. He then retreated up the Mississippi, hoping to meet reinforcements, or at least re-establish contact with Porter. He kept his coal boats lashed alongside, knowing that they would be needed if another steamer came down to join him. At 9.30 p.m. on 24 February, at Davis' Bend (named from the plantation of Jefferson Davis' brother) and within a few miles of his destination, he found himself being chased by the Confederate flotilla. After a desperate fight lasting almost an hour and a half, during which *Indianola* was repeatedly struck by the two rams, Brown ran his sinking boat aground, destroyed his guns, threw his signal books overboard and surrendered to the Confederate Commander James McCloskey.

Porter, in his report to Welles, described the loss of *Indianola* and *Queen of the West* within the space of twelve days as 'the most humiliating affair that has occurred during the rebellion ..., it almost disheartens me. I certainly had the right to expect that two vessels, carrying twelve guns, that had passed all the batteries at Vicksburg, Warrenton, Carthage, and other places on the river, could manage between them to take one old steamer or else have the wisdom and patriotism to destroy their vessels, even if they had to go with them'. The contemporary historian of the US Navy in the Civil War, Dr Boynton, a member of the faculty at the United States Naval Academy, Annapolis, commented on Porter's remarks that 'To blow one's self and crew into eternity, merely to prevent a vessel falling into the hands of an enemy, would make a very large demand on the patriotism of most men.' Nevertheless, he went on to blame Brown for failing to cast off the coal-boats that made *Indianola* difficult to manoeuvre and for not using his heavy guns against the rams. There was, he said, a lack not of courage, but of seamanship and skill.

Farragut was inclined to blame his foster-brother for the whole affair. 'Porter has allowed his boats to come down one at a time and they have been captured by the enemy, which compels me to go up and recapture the whole or be sunk in the attempt.' While the Union admirals raged, Confederate boats moved freely along the 240 miles of the Mississippi between Vicksburg and Port Hudson, men and supplies for the eastern Confederacy still came down the Red River, and Vicksburg itself, though periodically shelled and mortared, still kept the river closed to traffic from the North.

Porter fully realised that, if *Indianola* were salvaged and repaired, she would join *Queen of the West* and *William H. Webb* to give the Confederates a more formidable force on the river than they had had since the battle of Memphis. Unwilling to risk another boat to the Vicksburg batteries, he devised a deception plan that could be expected at least to delay the salvage work. He added a false prow and stern to an abandoned flatboat, and constructed a dummy forward turret of wood and canvas, with charcoal-blackened logs to represent guns. Aft of this were installed twin smoke-stacks made of pork barrels stacked one above the other, with smoke-pots, such as were used to protect cotton plants from frost, at their base. Towards the stern, more canvas and wood gave the impression of protected paddle wheels. The project was completed in twelve hours, at negligible cost.

On 25/26 February, the night following the loss of *Indianola*, the dummy gunboat was towed down to within range of Vicksburg and then, her smoke-pots ignited, released into the current. The batteries responded, wasting their charges and making no impression on a seemingly impregnable target 300-feet long. Below the city she ran aground on the Louisiana bank, but was pushed off by Union troops who had gathered to watch her progress. By dawn, she was again heading downstream, swept along by a five-knot current. She then encountered *Queen of the West* en route to Vicksburg. Seeing a large vessel approaching, with heavy smoke suggesting that her engines were at full speed and empty decks indicating that she was cleared for action, Commander McCloskey turned away to avoid a superior enemy. On his way back down the river, he passed the salvage crew aboard *Indianola* and warned them of what was following him. Together with *William H. Webb*, he then continued to the Red River. No one seems to have noticed that the unknown boat had neither a bow-wave to indicate that she was actually moving through the water, nor the wake that would have been created if she had been under power. The day passed without the strange vessel appearing, but, under orders from Vicksburg to burn *Indianola* rather than let her be recaptured, the Confederate officer in charge of the salvage party did so, after prudently unloading her liquor and wine stores. The next morning Confederate scouts found the dummy gunboat aground twelve miles upstream, and read the message that Porter, a master of psychological warfare, had painted on her false paddle boxes: 'DELUDED PEOPLE – CAVE IN'.

THE YAZOO PASS: FEBRUARY – MARCH 1863

Meanwhile, the progress of the Yazoo Pass expedition had slowed to a crawl. The Mississippi was still running rapidly through the blown levee, creating a strong current and sweeping logs and other debris along to foul the flotilla's paddle wheels and rudders. River boats require constant course corrections to avoid running aground and, like all vessels, must have steerage way to answer their helm. They had therefore to steam faster than the current that pushed them on, and though their speed through the water was slow, their speed relative to the bank was fast enough to make them difficult to handle in the narrow and tree-lined channel. If the boats slowed to avoid overhanging branches, they were swept into them by the current and their own momentum. If they maintained speed to keep steerage way and avoid going aground, they hit the trees with even greater force, wrecking their smoke-stacks, pilot houses and other upper works in the process. Navigation was made slower by the canopy of matted branches

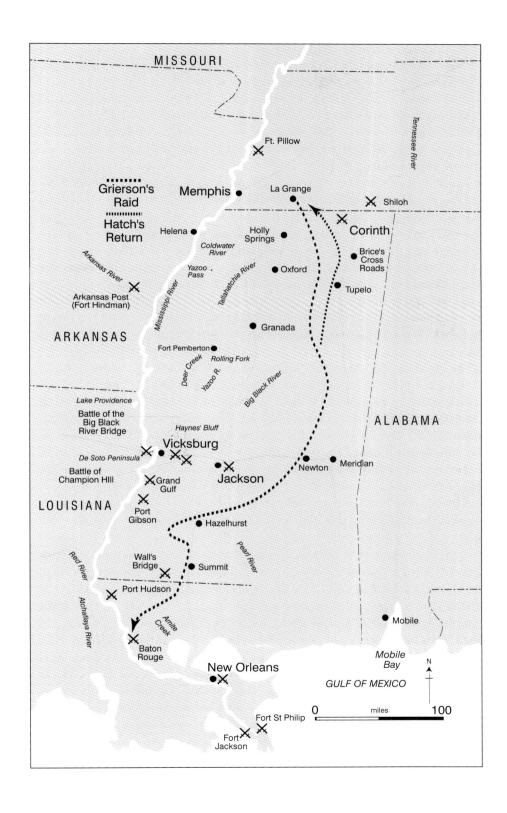

MISSOURI

Ft. Pillow

Grierson's Raid

Hatch's Return

Memphis ●

La Grange ●

Shiloh

Helena ●

Coldwater River

Holly Springs ●

Corinth ●

Brice's Cross Roads ●

Arkansas River

Yazoo Pass

Tallahatchie River

Oxford ●

Tupelo ●

Arkansas Post (Fort Hindman)

Mississippi River

Granada ●

ARKANSAS

Fort Pemberton ●

Deer Creek

Rolling Fork

Yazoo R.

Big Black River

ALABAMA

Lake Providence

Battle of the Big Black River Bridge

Haynes' Bluff

Vicksburg ●

De Soto Peninsula

Battle of Champion HIll

Grand Gulf

Jackson

Newton ●

Meridian ●

LOUISIANA

Port Gibson

Hazelhurst ●

Red River

Wall's Bridge

Summit ●

Pearl River

Atchafalaya River

Port Hudson

Mobile ●

Amite Creek

Baton Rouge

Mobile Bay

N

New Orleans ●

GULF OF MEXICO

0   miles   100

Fort St Philip

Fort Jackson

and vines that had grown in the years since the Yazoo Pass had been closed, and now shut out the daylight so that pilots could scarcely see their way through the channels. The waterway itself, despite the current, was continually blocked by log-jams that could take hours to deal with. When cleared and allowed to float downstream, the flotsam merely gathered again at the next snag. Meanwhile, the Confederates, so far from being taken by surprise, had assembled gangs of slaves from nearby plantations and added to the blockages by felling great trees across the waterway. Eventually a way was forced through, using a combination of the boats' machinery and man-hauling with teams of up to 500 soldiers at a time, and the flotilla emerged into the Coldwater River on 28 February with the cry of 'On to Vicksburg, boys, and no more trees to saw!'.

Anticipating this, troops from Vicksburg had constructed an earthwork, Fort Pemberton, on a low-lying neck of land above Greenwood, where the Tallahatchie and Yalobusha flow together to form the Yazoo. It was held by 2,000 men under Major General William Wing Loring, a 45-year-old veteran of the Seminole campaign in Florida and the Mexican War, where he had lost an arm. After resigning as colonel of the US Mounted Riflemen, he had fought for the Confederacy in West Virginia before being given command of a division in the Department of Mississippi and East Louisiana. His fort was armed with thirteen pieces of artillery, including a rifled 32-pdr sited to fire down the river along which the expedition was approaching. With nowhere to disembark their accompanying infantry, the gunboats advanced to the attack on 11 March. The Confederates had narrowed the channel by sinking a steamer as a block-ship, so that only *Chillicothe* and *De Kalb* could engage. Both were badly damaged by fire from the 32-pdr and retired with the loss of six men killed and twenty-five wounded. Watson Smith landed a 30-pdr from his command vessel, *Rattler*, and the soldiers brought up some field pieces to support the attack, which was renewed on 13 March. Following an action lasting over an hour and a half, *Chillicothe* withdrew after expending most of her ammunition and sustaining forty-four hits. *De Kalb* remained and continued to bombard the fort, which made no further reply, its own batteries also being out of ammunition, though the sailors did not know this. On 16 March the gunboats attacked again, only to be beaten back once more by the Confederate artillery.

Watson Smith reported that *Chillicothe*, a side-wheeler, was easier to manage in a narrow channel than the Eads gunboats, but that her armour, installed by fraudulent contractors, had proved unable to withstand the rifled cannon. His anxieties had been increased by a Southern voice shouting from the bank that the Confederates had a vessel ready to attack *Chillicothe*. He planned to meet boarders by ordering the crew below while her deck was swept by the fire of her consorts, but the threat turned out to be false. During his last attack he suffered a mental breakdown, and was subsequently evacuated for medical treatment. On 18 March command passed to Lieutenant James P. Foster, commanding the battered *Chillicothe*. The original scheme for blowing the levee had been devised by Lieutenant Colonel James Harrison Wilson, Grant's chief topographical engineer, who accompanied the expedition and had become increasingly frustrated by Watson Smith's cautious progress. In the hope that a rise in the level of water would flood out the defenders of low-lying Fort Pemberton, he proposed the blowing of a new breach, six miles above Helena. This was done, but, as Grant put it, 'It did not accomplish the desired result and Ross, with his fleet, started back.'

On 22 March they met Brigadier General Isaac Quinby coming with reinforcements from McPherson's XVII Corps. Quinby, the senior ranking officer, took command of the expedition and led it back through the cleared channels to reach Fort Pemberton the next day. *Chillicothe* went forward again and fired three shots to draw fire from the fort, but when none was returned, withdrew, the Confederates detonating a mine off her bow as she went. Foster told Quinby that the fort could not be taken without heavy siege guns. Quinby said he had some 24-pdrs with him and would send for more, but after twelve days' inaction, orders came from Grant to abandon the expedition. The Union forces, with the gunboats bringing up the rear, began their retreat on 4 April 1863 and returned to Helena six days later. Wilson blamed the Navy for allowing a single gun to stop the expedition in its tracks. Foster blamed the Army for not being ready to start on time. All agreed that if there had been no delays, they would have reached the Yazoo before a spade had been turned at Fort Pemberton.

Meanwhile, the two schemes to bypass Vicksburg on the Louisiana side of the river still continued. Of these, the De Soto canal met with a disaster on 8 March when the Mississippi, rising in response to continued heavy rain and the melting snows far upstream, broke through the protecting coffer dam, collapsed the canal's banks and filled the cut with silt and debris. The patient dredgers and diggers began again, but the tactical weakness of the scheme was revealed when the Confederates planted batteries opposite the canal's intended downstream mouth and forced the dredgers to keep out of range. Grant kept the work going in order to distract Confederate attention from his other movements, but the canal was eventually abandoned on 27 March. Upstream, the cut from the Mississippi into Lake Providence was opened on 18 March and caused flooding that filled the bayous and devastated the cotton plantations for miles around. The water road to the Red River lay open, but Grant had already decided that it was too long and too risky and withdrew the balance of McPherson's troops at the end of the month.

THE DEER CREEK EXPEDITION: MARCH 1863

Early in March, while the Yazoo Pass expedition was emerging into the Coldwater River, the indefatigable Porter made a personal reconnaissance into another set of waterways on the eastern side of the Mississippi. These ran from his anchorage at Milliken's Bend into Steele's Bayou. To the south this emptied into the Yazoo opposite the Chickasaw Bluffs and thus had no advantage over entering that river directly from the Mississippi. To the north, however, it joined Black Bayou, which linked with Deer Creek. Downstream, this reached the Yazoo opposite the batteries at Haynes' Bluff, but upstream it linked with another watercourse, Rolling Fork. Through this, steamboats could pass into the Big Sunflower River, and thence at last into the Yazoo well above Haynes' Bluff. This route would be 200 miles long, almost ten times the direct way from Milliken's Bend to Vicksburg, but the direct way was blocked by impregnable defences. By contrast, what Porter found in his scouting trip along the thirty miles up to Black Bayou was a waterway open to navigation. As a result of the broken levees at the Yazoo Pass and rainfall that was abnormally high even by local standards, there were nearly three fathoms of water where his gunboats required only one. The tops of drowned trees waved on the surface in a way that reminded him of the Sargasso Sea, while between them he saw channels wide enough to take a frigate.

On 14 March Porter took *Carondelet*, *Cincinnati*, *Louisville*, *Mound City* and *Pittsburg* into Steele's Bayou, accompanied by four mortar-boats and their tugs. Grant went with them for part of the way, and noted that, despite Porter's enthusiasm, the progress of the steamers was delayed by the number of sharp bends in the channel and by overhanging branches. The same high water level that allowed the boats to float in previously shallow places had the effect of decreasing the distance (known as air draught) between the highest part of the boats and the lowest part of obstacles under which they had to pass. Nevertheless, hoping that the Navy would win through, he returned to his headquarters and ordered Sherman to bring up a division from his XV Corps. Grant knew that Ross and the Yazoo Pass expedition had run into trouble at Fort Pemberton, but did not know when, or even if, the reinforcements sent by McPherson from Lake Providence would reach it. Once across the river, Sherman would be able either to support Porter or move to the aid of the Yazoo Pass expedition.

Sherman himself had long reached the conclusion that the De Soto canal was a waste of time, and was happy at the prospect of active operations. He took his men on large river transports to Eagle Bend, where they marched across the levee to re-embark on smaller steamboats in Steele's Bayou. Leading the way was the steamer *Diligence*, carrying the 8th Missouri Infantry. This unit included many river boatmen in its ranks, and was equipped with axes, saws and other pioneer tools for use in clearing the way for the high-sided transports. On 16 March they caught up with Porter in Deer Creek.

The gunboats had experienced more difficulty than their flag officer had expected. In his memoirs he described great trees that seemed to throw their branches round his approaching vessels like the hundred-handed giants of Greek mythology. All kinds of creatures, some natural tree-dwellers, others having climbed into the branches to escape the man-made floods, fell onto the decks and had to be swept overboard with brooms. Mice, squirrels, fledgling birds, rats, wild-cats, raccoons, snakes, lizards and insects of various types all had to be dealt with as the boats made their way along. Trees in the waterway could be pushed over and out of the way by the heavy ironclads, but, as had been the case in the Yazoo Pass, branches from those on the banks caught on their smoke-stacks, stays and other top hamper and, when cut through, crashed down onto the decks. The channel grew steadily narrower, shallower and more winding, so that at times the gunboats, as they followed one another, were each heading towards different points of the compass. *Cincinnati*, leading the way, found herself passing through a tunnel of flame and smoke when local plantation owners set fire to cotton stacked along the bank. In the smoke, she hit and carried away a wooden bridge, and subsequently used the same technique against other bridges that she met.

As with the Yazoo Pass expedition, Confederate sympathisers used gangs of slaves to fell trees across the waterway, which in places became scarcely wider than the gunboats themselves. Using blocks and tackles, steam and manpower, the sailors cleared the obstacles away, but the flotilla's slow progress was delayed still further. A mile or so short of the junction with Rolling Fork, they found the waterway choked by a floating mass of willow withies. A tug was sent forward to investigate and became entangled in them. *Carondelet* went to the rescue and became entangled in her turn. Despite desperate efforts by her crew, swarming over the side with saws, knives, cutlasses and chisels, she was unable to move either forward or back.

The movements of the flotilla had been followed without difficulty by the Confederate commanders and a steamer with troops from Vicksburg was already approaching Rolling Fork. Porter, having seen its smoke from three miles away, had already sent forward three hundred men with two howitzers to protect his intended route by establishing a battery on an old Indian mound. On 19 March the Confederates disembarked six rifled cannon, and opened fire on *Carondelet*, *Cincinnati* and the Indian mound. The battery replied but, heavily out-gunned, was soon abandoned. One of the mortar-boats threw a shell in the direction of the Confederate guns, which ceased firing, but Confederate sharpshooters, easily guided to the gunboats by their plumes of steam and coal-smoke, began to pick off any crewmen who appeared above decks. Through his spy-glass Porter saw another Confederate steamer arrive, crowded with infantry. At the same time, his boats were hit by a sudden surge of water, carrying with it a mass of fast-moving heavy fallen timber, that had to be fended off from their hulls, paddle wheels and steering gear. This was caused by the opening of the cut from the Mississippi opposite Helena, made with the intention of flooding out the defenders of Fort Pemberton. A friendly African-American told Grant that the troops from the Rolling Fork steamers had landed and were marching to cut off his retreat. The same man agreed to carry a message to Sherman, wrapped in a piece of tobacco leaf and hidden in his hair, outlining the gunboats' predicament and urging him to hurry to their aid. The rush of water had at least helped *Carondelet* and the tug get clear, so that during the night of 19/20 March the flotilla, unable to turn in the narrow channel, began to back down Deer Creek.

Porter's message reached Sherman at Hill's Plantation, at the confluence of Deer Creek and Black Bayou. The transports with his main force had not yet come up and the only troops so far landed were the 800 pioneers of the 8th Missouri Infantry with their brigade commander, Brigadier General Giles A. Smith. Sherman ordered them to move to Porter's aid without delay and paddled himself downstream in a canoe to hasten the transports. Finding the steamer *Silver Wave* just about to disembark the rest of Smith's brigade, he packed those already ashore into a coal barge and returned upstream through the forest with both boats, wrecking *Silver Wave*'s upper works in the process. They only managed to cover two and a half miles before dusk, after which Sherman decided that, despite the swampy ground, it would be quicker to march. In single file, lighted by hand-held candles, and guided only by the tapping of their drummers, the troops trudged on for another mile and a half, often up to their waists in water. At midnight on 20/21 March they bivouacked in a cotton field and then went on at dawn. They could see the tracks left by Smith's troops and, in Sherman's words, 'We could hear Porter's guns and knew that moments were precious. Being on foot myself, no man could complain, and we generally went at the double quick.'

Porter found his way back was blocked by a coal barge that, originally bringing up the rear, had sunk after being run into when the flotilla reversed course. Around him, the constant sound of Confederate axes and falling trees indicated that the flotilla would soon be completely trapped. With the boats unable to bring a gun to bear, every tree seemed to conceal an enemy marksman, making it impossible to work on raising the barge. Porter, not knowing if his message had got through, put his exhausted men on half rations and ordered that, if any vessel was in danger of being carried by boarders, it was to be destroyed by its crew. On his way to the flotilla, Smith encountered and defeated a body of 400 Confederate infantry engaged in felling trees across the waterway. He reached Porter during the afternoon of 21 March ('I was quite pleased to see him', said the flag officer in his report) and drove away the snipers, but, without artillery or supplies, could do no more than hold the banks while the barge was raised. The flotilla resumed its retreat on 22 March. *Louisville*, clearing a way through the forty heavy trees that, notwithstanding Smith's earlier success, still lay across the stream, came under Confederate artillery fire, but this time the gunboats could make an effective response. A 3,000-strong Confederate infantry force was reported nearby, but at noon Sherman reached the flotilla with two brigades, after covering twenty-one miles in six hours.

Porter, hearing his sailors' cheering, looked out to see Sherman himself on the bank a hundred yards away, now riding bareback on a decrepit nag his soldiers had found for him, with the troops coming through the cotton fields behind him. 'More welcome visitors he never had than the "boys in blue" on this occasion', wrote Grant many years later. Porter's own report, written at the time, said 'We fell in with General Sherman, who, hearing the firing, was hurrying to our support. I do not know when I was more pleased to see that gallant officer.' While the troops marched along the river-banks, the boats unshipped their rudders and made their way downstream to Hill's Plantation, which they had left eight days earlier. There they were able to turn and head back to the Mississippi, where the troops disembarked at Young's Point on 27 March. The boats resumed their station at the mouth of the Yazoo on the following day, to be joined a week later by those returning from the Yazoo Pass expedition.

Porter admitted that his expedition through the bayous had failed, but pointed to the great quantity of contraband cotton that he had taken on board (enough, he said, to pay for the building of a good gunboat), and another 20,000 bales that had been burnt by their owners on his approach. He withdrew the earlier reservations he had expressed about the utility of the gunboats, saying 'Never did those people expect to see ironclads floating where the keel of a flat-boat never passed.' At the same time, he admitted that the gunboats, in restricted waters, could not operate by themselves and that inter-service co-operation was essential. 'I never knew', he wrote, 'how helpless a thing an ironclad could be when unsupported by troops.'

THE BATTLE OF PORT HUDSON: MARCH 1863

To make up for the loss of *Indianola* and *Queen of the West*, Farragut took his own squadron past Port Hudson, commanded by the Confederate Major General Franklin Gardner, on 14 March. As well as his flagship *Hartford*, he had the 22-gun *Richmond*, the 10-gun *Monongahela* and the 22-gun *Mississippi*, all fully-rigged seagoing steamships. With them were the seagoing screw gunboats *Albatross*, *Genesee*, *Kineo*, the shallow-draught side-wheeler *Sachem*, four mortar-schooners and the river gunboat *Essex*, which had joined him after her duel with *Arkansas*. It was intended that troops from Baton Rouge, provided by Major General Nathaniel

Rear-Admiral David Glasgow Farragut, with his chief of staff, Captain Percival Drayton, on the deck of his flagship, the steam-sloop *Hartford*.

P. Banks (Major General 'Beast' Butler's successor in command of the Army of the Gulf) would create a diversion on the landward side, while the squadron ran the batteries during the night. *Albatross*, *Genesee* and *Kineo* respectively were lashed alongside *Hartford*, *Richmond* and *Monongahela*, on the port quarter, this being the side away from the batteries. The gunboats were assigned according to their speed, with *Richmond*, the slowest ship, being given *Genesee*, the fastest and most powerful of the gunboats. *Mississippi* and *Sachem*, the two side-wheelers, were to run singly. Farragut's plan was that, if any of the big ships were disabled, the gunboats would provide sufficient motive power to go on, if their captains thought they could get by, or else drop back out of range of Port Hudson's fifty guns. If the gunboats or singletons were disabled, they were to use their sails or light club anchors to control their descent downstream. *Essex*, armoured but under-powered, and the vulnerable mortar-schooners were left behind to engage the batteries as soon as the ships came under fire.

The attack got off to a bad start when Banks, true to his nick-name of 'Nothing Positive', sent a boat to say that he could not provide the diversion that Farragut had requested. The signal to get under way (two red lantern lights hung over the stern) was made after nightfall, but two ships were late in getting into line and it was another hour before the squadron began to move. Meanwhile the Confederate gunners, who had had all day to observe the ships raising steam and preparing for action and who were already alerted by the mortars' ranging shots, took post to receive them. One battery, equipped with a furnace, prepared to produce red-hot shot, the standard weapon of coastal artillery against wooden ships. Fires were started on the Louisiana bank to silhouette the ships as they moved up and the first shots were exchanged at about 11 p.m. As with the previous actions at Vicksburg, a combination of night-time mist from the river and smoke from the shore fires, the steamers' smoke-stacks and the heavy artillery of both sides soon blanketed the channel. *Hartford*, leading the way, was controlled by her pilot from the mizen-top with the aid of an acoustic tube. Though fully exposed to enemy fire, he was above the smoke and thus able to con the ship through the darkness. Nevertheless, as she rounded the bend by the upper batteries, she was caught by the current and, hampered by *Albatross* lashed alongside, spun completely round to starboard and was swept back downstream to hit the Port Hudson bank. With her own engines full ahead, and those of *Albatross* full astern, she was turned to port and once more headed upstream. Farragut's young son Loyall, acting as his signal-officer, flinched from the hail of lead and iron, but was told by his battle-hardened father, 'Don't duck, my son, there is no use in trying to dodge God Almighty,' He survived, to be mentioned in dispatches with the other officers, but, after passing the batteries, the admiral looked for the rest of his squadron in vain.

At twenty minutes past midnight, *Richmond*, second in the line, received a hit in the engine-room which reduced pressure and filled the ship with steam. Even with *Genesee* alongside, she could not make headway against the current, and became an easy target for the shore batteries. With three men killed and twelve wounded, her captain turned back and anchored out of range, after firing 132 rounds of various natures. *Monongahela*, following *Richmond*, ran aground with *Kineo* (both vessels having already had their rudders damaged) and remained stationary under heavy fire for twenty minutes before getting off. After going down with the current, *Monongahela* turned and again tried to pass the batteries. An over-heated crank-pin stopped one of her engines, so that she became unmanageable and, with six men killed and twenty-one wounded, drifted back downstream. After rescuing *Monongahela*, *Kineo*'s own engines gave out, but she was able to come safely to anchor.

Mississippi, fourth in line, had been scarcely able to see through the smoke of all those ahead and had nearly fired on the disabled *Richmond* as she passed on the way down. With her engines at maximum revolutions in an attempt to catch up with *Monongahela*, which had disappeared in the smoke and darkness, her pilot missed the approaching bend of the river, and the ship ran hard aground with the full impact of her 1,700 tons. After half an hour with her engines running full astern, the engine-room crew had to let off steam to prevent the boilers exploding. The white plumes so created gave the shore batteries a perfect aiming mark, and after repeated hits, her commanding officer decided to save his crew and burn the ship to prevent capture. The crew was got onto the bank or into the boats, and *Richmond*, relieved of the weight of nearly three hundred men, and possibly dislodged by the continued impact of enemy shot, refloated herself and, still on fire, drifted downstream to blow up with a shattering explosion. Most of her crew survived, but three officers, fifty-two seamen and eight marines were killed or missing.

Farragut, exchanging fire with the batteries at Grand Gulf and Warrenton as he passed, took *Hartford* and *Albatross* on to reach the anchorage below Vicksburg on 18 March. He established communications overland with Grant and Porter and asked for gunboats to be sent down to join him. Boats with coal and provisions passed down during the night to replenish his depleted bunkers and stores, but there were no gunboats to send. Seven of Porter's ironclads were at Fort Pemberton and another five, under his personal command, were steaming through the bayous in his attempt to reach the Yazoo. Brigadier General Alfred Ellet offered two of his rams instead. On 23 March *Lancaster*, commanded by the general's nephew, Lieutenant Colonel John A. Ellet, and *Switzerland*, under Lieutenant Colonel Charles R. Ellet (*Queen of the West*'s former captain) started down the river. *Lancaster* was hit thirty times and sank. *Switzerland*, with a shot through her boiler, drifted downstream out of control until she was rescued by *Hartford*. Charles R. Ellet was subsequently assigned to infantry duty with the Marine brigade, and command of *Switzerland*, after she had been repaired, was given to his cousin John A. Ellet. This officer had been threatened by Porter with a court-martial for insubordination, arising from his habit of constantly referring the orders of the flag officer (under whose control the rams came for operational purposes) to Brigadier General Ellet. Once below Vicksburg, his relations with Farragut, under whose command he now came, were entirely correct.

Yet again the jubilant citizens and garrison of Vicksburg could celebrate a victory over the baffled Yankees. Upstream, Porter and the once feared gunboats had been forced into ignominious retreat. At Vicksburg itself, Ellet had lost the ram *Lancaster*. Downstream, Farragut had lost *Mississippi* at Port Hudson and, after reaching Vicksburg, retired from the city for a third time. The Confederate flag still flew proudly over Vicksburg's defences, and the great river was still closed to Union traffic.

THE MARCH DOWN THE RIVER: APRIL 1863

Grant, Porter and Sherman all spoke well of one another in their reports, though their superiors in Washington were less satisfied with what had been achieved. Gideon Welles at the Department of the Navy commented that the results of Porter's schemes did not justify the losses suffered. Lincoln, however, still had faith in Grant and, when pressed to replace him with McClernand, said 'I cannot spare the man; he fights.' Nevertheless, Northern newspapers carried reports of Grant's intemperance and complained that he was merely digging ditches instead of advancing on Vicksburg. Lincoln's Secretary of War, Edwin Stanton, heard tales that Grant was idle (he was certainly slow in keeping Washington informed of his activities) and unfit for command. At the beginning of April he sent his own confidential agent, the lecturer and newspaperman Charles Anderson Dana, to join Grant's staff and send back daily reports. In fact, this proved of benefit to Grant, as the two men got on well together, and Dana's reports relieved Grant from the need to write his own.

On 1 April, Farragut, with *Hartford*, *Albatross* and *Switzerland*, took station at the mouth of the Red River. From there he was able to prevent the Confederates using this waterway to bring supplies from Texas or to reinforce south-western Louisiana, where Banks, supported by four light gunboats from Farragut's command, had begun to advance up the Atchafalaya River on 12 April. This waterway leaves the Red River a short distance above its confluence with the Mississippi and then flows south to reach the sea, through a maze of lakes and salt-marshes, some miles west of New Orleans. In a series of engagements, the outnumbered Confederates were driven northwards and CSS *Queen of the West* was blown up to prevent her being re-captured. The light gunboats *Arizona* and *Estrella* entered the Red River from the Atchafalaya and went down to join Farragut at its confluence with the Mississippi.

Grant had begun his own offensive on 31 March. Abandoning any idea of reaching Vicksburg from the Yazoo, he decided to move his army from Milliken's Bend, down the western bank of the Mississippi, to New Carthage, Louisiana, opposite the confluence with the Big Black River. To evade the batteries at Vicksburg and Warrenton, he opened one more waterway, using labour and dredgers from the abandoned De Soto project. It ran from Duckport, below Milliken's Bend, through a series of bayous on the western side of the river to Richmond, Louisiana, and thence back into the Mississippi at New Carthage, twenty miles below Vicksburg, but well above the batteries at Grand Gulf. The advantage of this route was that the waterway was flanked by roads running along the top of the levees. With the advent of dry weather, the roads would emerge from the flooded countryside to allow the movement of troops, guns and wagons.

Grant calculated that he had sufficient steamers and barges to move 20,000 men along the forty-mile waterway in a single lift. The boats would carry the artillery and combat supplies. Regiments for whom there was no room on board would march to New Carthage overland. Once there, the army would need the aid of the Navy to cross the river. Grant knew that Farragut had only *Hartford* and *Albatross* under his immediate command and that even these, having gone below the newly strengthened Confederate batteries at Grand Gulf, were not available to help. On 2 April he appealed to Porter, saying, 'I would, admiral, therefore renew my request for running the blockade at as early a day as possible.'

On the Vicksburg side, Pemberton reported on 11 April 1863 that most of the Union troops at Milliken's Bend had gone. His supposition was that Grant had retreated to Memphis, which would have been the conventionally correct military course. Sherman had argued for it on the grounds that even if Grant's army reached the east bank, it would be between the two strongholds of Vicksburg and Port Hudson, with the river between it and its base, a position that an enemy might have had to manoeuvre for months to bring about. General Joseph E. Johnston, commanding the Confederate Department of the West, agreed with Pemberton and Sherman. Anticipating that Grant would subsequently march his army eastwards from Memphis, he ordered Pemberton to send an infantry division to Bragg's Army of Tennessee. This effectively returned the reinforcements sent by Bragg (on the direct orders of Jefferson Davis) to Pemberton in December 1862, when Grant had been advancing from Holly Springs.

With daily working parties of two thousand men from McClernand and another thousand from Sherman, the Duckport canal, forty feet wide and seven feet deep, was begun on 29 March. McClernand led the way southwards, his pioneers felling trees to lay corduroy roads and pulling down wooden buildings to make bridges and ferries. Encountering only token resistance, they reached New Carthage within a week and completed the canal within a fortnight. On 13 April the navigation was opened and a small steamer with some barges started for New Carthage. In the event, they were the only vessels to get through, as the Mississippi then began to fall to its summer level and the canal, reduced to a string of muddy ditches, had to be abandoned. Slowly, the drowned tracks appeared, but horse-drawn road vehicles could move only a fraction of what could be carried by water transport. Grant now needed not only the gunboats, but the transport steamers.

Porter had promised Grant that the necessary boats would be sent, but warned him that, once below Vicksburg, they would never be able to return. With their heavy armour and engines worn-out by many months in commission, the speed of the gunboats against the current would be scarcely two knots, making them an easy target for the shore batteries. The transports could run faster, but would be

Grant as a lieutenant general with his staff during the western campaign, as portrayed by late nineteenth-century artist H. A. Ogden.

smashed into match-wood as soon as the gunners found their range. Going downstream, the current would give them extra speed, but, even travelling at night, they would still be vulnerable. The transports belonged to the Army rather than the Navy, but Grant readily agreed to Porter's suggestion that his sailors, rather than the soldiers, should prepare them for the coming action. To conceal their boiler fires and protect the boilers, Porter packed the boats with hay-bales and sacks of grain (which would anyway be wanted by the army) and the cotton-bales which had become a standard form of defensive cladding.

After nightfall on 16 April they got under way. The gunboats *Benton* (wearing Porter's flag), *Lafayette*, *Louisville*, *Mound City*, *Pittsburg*, *Carondelet* and the newly joined *Tuscumbia* formed a line at fifty-yard intervals, staggered so that if one boat were to be stopped, the next astern would not run into her. All deck lights were out and the boiler fires well ignited, to produce the least possible amount of smoke. As they neared the batteries, they diverted their exhausts into the paddle wheels, to silence the characteristic puc-a-puc sound of a steamboat under way, and hugged the shore so that, in the dark, their hulls would not be seen against the bank-side trees. Guns were loaded with shell or grape-shot and set at a range of 900 yards. Each boat had a coal-barge on her starboard side, lashed so that it could be quickly cut adrift in case of emergency. The small steamer *General Price* (captured at the battle of Memphis) and one of the Ellet rams were lashed along the starboard sides of the leading boats, and the transports *Forest Queen*, *Silver Wave* and *Henry Clay*, towing twelve fully-laden coal-barges between them, brought up the rear. Aboard the steamer *Von Phul*, Grant, with his staff and his family, joined by McClernand and his new bride, watched them go.

Within Vicksburg, the disappearance of Grant's army had cheered citizens and soldiers alike. The same warm weather that was drying out the route to New Carthage encouraged the ladies to put on their spring clothes and emerge, as a visiting journalist noted, like April flowers. Officers and their belles prepared for a cotillion ball to be held in the evening of 16 April. The ball began, but was disturbed by the sound of artillery as the flotilla was detected. The boats immediately increased speed and during the next hour and a half there was a general exchange of gunfire. At the first alarm, Confederate volunteers crossed the river in small rowing boats to kindle fires on the opposite bank and illuminate the approaching vessels. Some Union pilots, confused by the lights, missed their way through the shoals, and had to turn their boats round under fire. These eccentric manoeuvres helped spoil the aim of the Confederate gun-layers, whose difficulty in judging the distance of moving targets at night was increased by the flash and smoke of artillery fire from both sides.

Nevertheless, they scored five hits on *Benton*, and nine on *Lafayette*, the next in line. *General Price*, twice reported on fire, was safely cast off after passing the batteries. *Lafayette*'s coal barge was sunk by a shot in the bows and two others were lost. Every vessel was hit, some many times, but only the unarmoured transports suffered severe damage. *Forest Queen* was hit on the water-line and stopped below the city. *Henry Clay* was disabled and abandoned by her crew. After being set on fire by a shell, she drifted along, a burning wreck watched with awe by spectators from both sides, to run aground at New Carthage. Her pilot took refuge on a plank and was rescued by Sherman, who had gone out in a rowing boat to greet Porter's arrival. Ashore, Union soldiers on the road to New Carthage heard the gunfire and guessed they would find the Navy waiting for them. With the dawn, Grant made the long ride down to congratulate Porter in person.

LAND WARFARE
THE APPROACH TO VICKSBURG: APRIL – MAY 1863

At New Carthage, Grant decided that although there was too little water in the canal for his barges, there was still too much on the land for the speedy movement of an army of 30,000 men. He therefore decided to by-pass the town, and rejoin the Mississippi about ten miles further downstream, at Perkins's Plantation, opposite Davis's Bend. This made the march from Milliken's Bend thirteen miles longer, but offered drier going than the approaches to New Carthage. Where there were streams to be bridged, the pioneers again set to work and along the way built four fixed bridges, two of them being more than 600 feet long. Grant later spoke proudly of the ingenuity of his soldiers, most of them from the farms and settlements of the Mid-West. During the entire move just one gun, a 32-pdr, was lost, when it broke through their only pontoon bridge.

With the army there moved not only its integral unit transport (one wagon for every company, fifty-five for every brigade), but also its supply trains, the commissariat wagons moving up and down the road from Milliken's Bend to bring a total of ten days' rations. Food had to be carried not only for men but for horses. The hay and grain on which the teams depended was as essential as oil and petrol would become when horses were replaced by the internal combustion engine. A horse, like a mechanically propelled vehicle, will eventually consume all that it can haul, so that replenishment points have to be set up and maintained along the way. Grant's logisticians had to keep these supplied, so placing further traffic on the muddy road while the army and the ration wagons pressed on.

To mask the advance down the west side of the Mississippi, Grant launched a series of raids on the east side, far inland of Vicksburg. On 18 April an infantry brigade was sent from Memphis to threaten the Confederate base at Panola, Mississippi. Another force went by rail from La Grange, Tennessee, to Coldwater and from there marched against Confederate positions on the Tallahatchie River east of Panola. At the same time Brigadier General Grenville H. Dodge moved from Corinth along the Tennessee River to Tuscumbia, Alabama. On 26 April he was joined by 1,700 cavalrymen, mounted mostly on mules, and led by Colonel Abel H. Streight, 51st Indiana Infantry. Streight then headed across Alabama, hoping to rejoin the Union lines at Rome, Georgia, but was soon pursued by two regiments of Confederate cavalry under Nathan Bedford Forrest. After a running fight, Streight's men, too exhausted to feed their mounts or even stay awake in combat, were trapped and forced to surrender on 3 May.

GRIERSON'S RAID: 17 APRIL – 2 MAY 1863

Meanwhile, the 1st Brigade of the 1st Cavalry Division in Hurlbut's XVI Corps rode out of La Grange on 17 April. This brigade was made up of the 6th and 7th

Illinois Cavalry, the 2nd Iowa Cavalry, and Battery K of the 1st Illinois Light Artillery, a total of 1,700 men, commanded by Colonel Benjamin Henry Grierson, 6th Illinois Cavalry, a 35-year-old former professional musician and music-teacher. As well as the general aim of confusing the Confederates as to Grant's intentions and drawing troops away from the Mississippi, he had the specific task of disrupting the rail communications on which Vicksburg depended for re-supply and reinforcements. Taking what military supplies they could use and burning what they could not, and with some men (despite Grierson's orders) unable to resist the temptation to loot private property, these horse soldiers covered the thirty miles south to Ripley in twenty-four hours. There Colonel Edward Hatch, 2nd Iowa Cavalry, was detached with his regiment to give the impression that the raid was intended to cut the Mobile and Ohio Railroad, twenty miles away to the east. Grierson continued south and forded the upper Tallahatchie upstream of New Albany to bivouac at Chiwapa Creek, some thirty-five miles south of Ripley, where Hatch rejoined him.

Unfit men and horses, together with such prisoners of war as they had taken, were formed into a column about two hundred strong and sent westwards to Oxford to create the illusion that Grierson was returning to La Grange by that route. Grierson then continued south to skirt Houston, Mississippi, under cover of a diversionary attack on the town, before making camp twelve miles beyond it. On 21 April Hatch was again detached to the east as if to threaten the Mobile and Ohio Railroad. Before leaving, his regiment rode over the tracks left by the rest of the brigade as it moved south, and drove his single gun in circles to give the impression of a whole battery. Colonel Clark R. Barteau reached the scene with a Confederate cavalry brigade, interpreted Hatch's tracks as those of the entire column and rode in pursuit. He made contact with Hatch later that day, but was unable to prevent him from turning north to pass through Tupelo, destroying communications and 'contraband' *matériel* as he went. On 24 April, still forty-five miles south-east of La Grange, Hatch was brought to battle, but crossed Camp Creek and burnt the bridge behind him. Barteau, his horses exhausted and his troopers out of ammunition, was forced to let the raiders escape. They reached La Grange in safety two days later, accompanied by numerous runaway slaves and captured livestock.

The night before Hatch escaped over Camp Creek, Grierson led his main force through Decatur, heading for Newton on the Southern Railroad. The advance party rode into the town in the morning of 24 April just as two trains arrived laden with combat supplies for the Confederate Army. The trains were diverted into a siding and set ablaze, but the sound of ammunition exploding in the burning freight-cars led Grierson, coming up with the rest of his command, to suppose that there was fighting. He rode rapidly forward expecting to take part in a rescue action, but discovered that the main hazard was from the Confederate whiskey that his troopers had removed from one of the trains and hastily transferred to their canteens.

Each of the two regiments then moved along the tracks on each side of the station. Rails were torn up, heated in fires fuelled by the wooden sleepers and, when malleable, run against standing telegraph poles. Bent into the shape of hairpins, they were useless until they could be re-forged in the South's already over-strained steel-mills. Telegraph poles were felled and their wires repeatedly cut. Wooden bridges were burnt and rolling stock was blown up, with the fragments strewn along the line to delay the work of repair.

The brigade then headed westwards, preceded by scouts dressed in nondescript 'butternut'-coloured clothing. This enabled them to pass as Confederates and on one occasion to be given refreshment by Southern ladies as they were mistakenly welcomed into a fine plantation house. On 26 April, pushing on through heavy rain and flooded roads, they reached the swollen Pearl River and began to cross, using a small ferry captured in a *ruse de guerre*. Grierson and his officers were invited to an excellent breakfast at a nearby plantation house, 'the ladies all smiles', as he later recorded. He supposed they thought he was leading a force of Alabama cavalry to the rescue of Vicksburg, though it seems questionable that they could not tell the Union's blue uniforms from the Confederate Army's grey, and possibly their gracious entertainment was intended to occupy him while they sent word of his presence.

Despite the depredations of his men, Grierson was winning the reluctant admiration of many of his Southern foes. One lady, as he passed her plantation, told him that if the South were ever forced back into the Union, and Grierson ran for President, her husband (at that time away serving with the Confederate Army) would have the choice of either voting for him or being divorced. Southern generals, basing their judgement on events in the war thus far, were taken aback to find mid-western farm boys assuming the daring cavalry role that men from the land of cavaliers and cotton had regarded as peculiarly their own.

During the afternoon of 27 April Grierson reached Hazelhurst, fourteen miles west of the crossing. From there he telegraphed Pemberton's headquarters with the disinformation that the Yankees had been unable to get over the Pearl River as the ferry had been destroyed (something Pemberton would have expected to be done as the raiders approached) and moved off to the north-east. He then continued in the opposite direction with little opposition, as the Confederates on his western flank were occupied by the infantry columns from Memphis and Coldwater, those behind him had been pursuing Hatch, and those on the east were drawn away by the movements of Dodge's infantry and Streight's raid, which was then just getting under way.

Pemberton, most of whose cavalry had been sent by Johnston to reinforce Bragg in the previous January, was unable to obtain firm information about what was going on in northern Mississippi. On 22 April, two days before the destruction of Newton station, he telegraphed Johnston to report that the enemy were raiding deep into Mississippi and asking for cavalry support. The next day he sent a similar message to Jefferson Davis: 'I have so little cavalry in this department that I am compelled to divert a portion of my infantry to meet raids in northern Mississippi.' Johnston had already ordered back to Vicksburg the infantry division that had just left to reinforce Bragg, but, fearing a Union offensive in Tennessee, decided that no cavalry could be spared. On 27 April, with Grierson having been located at Hazelhurst, Pemberton reported to Johnston that, no matter how necessary cavalry was to the Army of Tennessee, it was indispensable in Mississippi. He could not, he said, defend every railway station with infantry and, by recalling Barteau's brigade from northern Mississippi, he had been forced to leave that sector unprotected.

On 30 April Jefferson Davis raised with Johnston the question of Pemberton's shortage of cavalry, to be told 'About three thousand of General Bragg's cavalry, beyond the Tennessee, are employing about twelve thousand Federal troops from Mississippi. General Pemberton has been so informed twice.' These troops were those that had been sent to counter the Union movements in northern Alabama, including the brigade under Nathan Bedford Forrest, at that time hard on the heels of Streight's raid.

With no help coming from Johnston, and Barteau still far away, Pemberton deployed what forces he had. Troops were sent to defend the bridges of the Big Black and so guard Vicksburg's vital supply line. A mounted infantry regiment was deployed to prevent Grierson retreating the way he had come, though as he had destroyed all the bridges and ferries on his line of march, this option was not really open. Loring's division at Meridian, the major railway junction eighty miles east of Jackson, blocked any escape in that direction. In the south, the Louisiana Legion was ordered out from Port Hudson. To the west, a regiment of cavalry under Colonel Wirt Adams was sent from Grand Gulf on 27 April and surprised Grierson's pickets at Union Church the following day.

Grierson drove off this attack but realised that other columns would be closing in on him. Still with no news of whether Grant had crossed the river, he abandoned any idea of joining forces and decided to head straight for the Union lines at Baton Rouge, a hundred miles away through Confederate-held territory. He destroyed the New Orleans and Jackson Railroad between Brookhaven and Bogue Chitto Stations on 29 April and, after a two-hour rest at Summit, turned westwards. Following a back-country route through flooded woods and farm tracks, he reached Wall's Bridge across the Tickfaw River on 1 May. There, three companies of the 9th Louisiana Partisan Rangers ambushed his advance guard, but the way was cleared by his artillery and a mounted charge across the river. Men too badly wounded to ride were entrusted to the chivalry of their Southern pursuers and left behind as the brigade hurried on to re-cross the winding Tickfaw at Edwards Bridge.

At Clinton, Louisiana, a unit sent down from Port Gibson was confident that Grierson was at last trapped. Believing they were well ahead of him, the officers attended a ball given in their honour by the jubilant citizens. While they danced, the Union troops marched through the night to cross Amite Creek a few miles away at Williams Bridge. During the morning of 2 May, with the Confederates two hours behind them, they started to ride the last thirty miles towards Baton Rouge, the exhausted men falling asleep in their saddles and their hungry horses straying from the flooded road to snatch a mouthful of grass. Followed by large numbers of former plantation slaves, Grierson at last reached the outposts of Baton Rouge and, after convincing the New Englanders that this was not a Confederate trick and that he really had come all the way from La Grange, led his command into the town in the mid-afternoon. He reported that he had ridden more than 600 miles in sixteen days, inflicted 600 enemy casualties for the loss of twenty-six, and destroyed between 50 and 60 miles of railway lines as well as an immense amount of Confederate government property. More importantly, he had achieved Grant's aim of drawing Pemberton's attention away from the Mississippi.

THE PASSAGE OF THE MISSISSIPPI: APRIL 1863

When Grierson left La Grange, Grant was on his way back to Milliken's Bend from his visit to New Carthage. There, he ordered McPherson's XVII Corps to follow McClernand to Perkins' Plantation. As the road was inadequate for the number of wagons needed to carry rations for so many men, he turned again to the river-boats above Vicksburg. Six steamers were each loaded with one day's rations for a hundred thousand men and protected with cotton and hay-bales. Each towed two barges alongside, carrying more rations and providing the steamers with additional further protection. A problem arose when, mindful of the spectacular fate of *Henry Clay*, most of the crews, who were not enlisted personnel but ordinary river boatmen whose boats had been chartered by the Army, declined to go with them. Only two captains and one complete crew were willing to remain aboard. Grant called for volunteers from any of his troops who had experience of the Western rivers and large numbers of riverboat captains, pilots, mates, engineers and deck-hands came forward.

On the night of 22–23 April the boats drifted silently down with the current until detected by Vicksburg's waiting gunners and then went to full revolutions. Grant, in *Von Phul*, watched them without a word, knowing that, if they did not get through, his entire plan of campaign would have to be abandoned. *Tigress*, in the lead, was hit thirty times and sank after passing the batteries, her crew escaping on floating wreckage. About half of the barges and their much-needed cargoes were lost, but despite being badly damaged, the remaining five steamers reached New Carthage. Some were fit only to be towed, but Grant now had provisions for his men and horses and enough steamers and smaller boats, collected from every creek and landing-stage below Vicksburg, to carry them over the river.

Grant's first intention had been to cross directly from his new assembly area at Perkins's Plantation, but scouting boats reported that there was no landing-place on the far bank from which an army might move. The nearest practicable crossing was twenty-two miles down river, held on the eastern side by the

Confederates on the bluffs at Grand Gulf. Immediate action was delayed by McClernand's decision to hold a review of his Corps for Governor Richard Yates of Illinois, who was at that time visiting Grant's headquarters. Eventually, on 27 April, 10,000 of McClernand's men, all that could be packed aboard the steamers, were taken down to Hard Times Landing, on the Louisiana bank just above Grand Gulf. The remainder, followed by McPherson's XVII Corps, continued their march in unpleasantly warm weather, along the improved but still muddy roads, made worse by the same rains that were affecting Grierson's distant raiders. Grant's plan now was for the gunboats to silence Grand Gulf's three forts, which mounted thirteen heavy guns with a field battery in support, so that the transports could go past. Covered by the gunboats, the troops would then disembark at the nearest landing-place and carry Grand Gulf by storm.

Early on 29 April Porter led his flotilla down to the attack. *Louisville*, *Carondelet*, *Mound City* and *Pittsburg* engaged the two upstream forts, while *Tuscumbia*, *Benton* (the flagship) and *Lafayette* ran past them to engage the fort downstream.

Porter's Union fleet making the dangerous run down the Mississippi past Vicksburg.

The defences of Grand Gulf were not as formidable as those of Vicksburg, and Porter, though expecting that the gunboats would be 'knocked about a bit', was willing to accept the risks. With the river swollen by the recent rain and its six-knot stream distorted by powerful eddies, the boats proved so difficult to manage that some were swept completely round as they tried to keep station opposite their targets. At times they drifted to within a few yards of the shore and their crews opened fire with muskets and revolvers. *Lafayette* fired 258 heavy rounds and was hit forty times. *Tuscumbia* fired 429 rounds and suffered eighty-one hits. *Benton* fired 347 rounds and was hit forty-seven times. The flotilla suffered a total of eighteen men killed and fifty-seven wounded during an engagement that lasted for more than four hours. Grant watched the battle from an unarmed tug, reasoning that the batteries would not bother to shoot at a small vessel when they were under fire themselves, and then went aboard *Benton* to confer with Porter. A battle-hardened soldier, he recorded that the sight of the mangled and dying men that met his eye as he boarded the flagship was sickening. The action was broken off and most of the boats then returned to Hard Times to tie up alongside the bank. *Tuscumbia*, like her sister-ship *Chillicothe* before Fort Pemberton, found that the 9in pine backing to her armour was inadequate to hold it in place

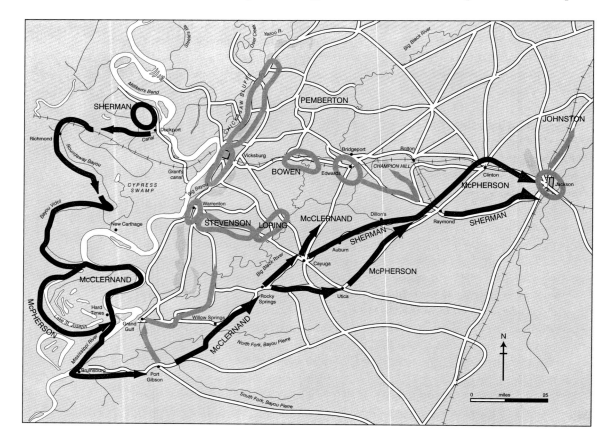

against rifled artillery fire. With her port engine out of action, she lacked the power to stem the current and dropped downstream.

McClernand was now ordered to disembark his troops at Hard Times and march along the west bank while the gunboats and empty transports ran past Grand Gulf during the night. Grant at first thought that the next landing-place was at Rodney, nine miles downstream from Grand Gulf. An African-American with knowledge of the area told him that, if he crossed from Dishroon's Plantation, a mere three miles away, he could get ashore at Bruinsburg, from where a good road led inland to Port Gibson. Porter reached this point without loss and offered Grant his gunboats as additional troop transports. At dawn on 30 April the inhabitants of Bruinsburg awoke to find their river front crowded with Union vessels, the decks black, or rather, as Grant said, blue, with Union soldiers. During the day a total of 23,000 men, comprising McClernand's XIII Corps, followed by two brigades of McPherson's XVII Corps, disembarked without opposition.

Grant had already discussed with Sherman the idea of making a feint up the Yazoo while the rest of the army crossed the Mississippi, warning him that it would be reported in the Northern press as if his troops had failed there a second time. Sherman gave Grant his full support, and told his men to disregard the newspapers. During 30 April and 1 May, while Grant pushed inland from Bruinsburg, Sherman went up the Yazoo with a division of infantry in troop transports, escorted by those gunboats that had not gone downstream with Porter. While the steamers made as much noise and smoke as they could, the troops spread out on the decks, then ostentatiously disembarked out of range of the Confederate batteries. They then marched under cover of the riverside trees to re-embark where they could not be seen and, concealed below deck, were carried down-river only for the boats to return and repeat the process.

Observing the landings from Haynes' Bluff was Major General Carter L. Stevenson, a 46-year-old Virginian and a graduate of the USMA, West Point. A veteran of the Seminole, Mexican, Mormon and Indian frontier campaigns, he had fought for the Confederacy in Virginia and Kentucky before being assigned to Vicksburg late in 1862. He sent word to Pemberton's headquarters at Jackson that large numbers of enemy had landed, in such force as had never been seen before at Vicksburg, and that reinforcements were urgently needed. Pemberton had just sent 3,000 men out of the city to reinforce the 32-year-old Brigadier General John S. Bowen at Grand Gulf. Bowen, a graduate of the USMA, West Point, and a former captain in the US Mounted Riflemen, had reported the battle with the gunboats and the presence of numerous enemy troops at Hard Times, clear indications of a possible attack from that direction. Before the troops from Vicksburg could reach him, they were recalled in response to Stevenson's message, giving them a pointless forced march of thirty miles in each direction. While the exhausted Confederate infantry staggered back into Vicksburg, the phantom menace of Sherman's expedition disappeared down the

Yazoo, leaving nothing but a trail of smoke. Having lured the reinforcements away from Grand Gulf, Sherman hurried down the wagon road to Perkins's Plantation, where a new and well-defended supply base was being built up.

In a famous passage from his Memoirs, Grant summed up his position. 'Vicksburg was not yet taken it is true, nor were the defenders demoralized by any of our previous moves. I was now in the enemy's country, with a vast river and the stronghold of Vicksburg between me and my base of supplies. But I was on dry ground on the same side of the river as the enemy. All the campaigns, labors, hardships and exposures from the month of December previous to this time that had been made and endured were for the accomplishment of this sole object.' After establishing his bridgehead and issuing ammunition and two days' rations (with orders that they were to last five), he sent McClernand's Corps forward during the night of 30 April/1 May to secure the road to Port Gibson. In the early hours of the morning, about four miles short of the town, they made contact with Confederate troops under Brigadier General Martin E. Green, whom Bowen had sent down from Grand Gulf as soon as he saw the transports run past his batteries.

THE BATTLE OF PORT GIBSON: 1 MAY 1863

During the ensuing battle, Bowen deployed most of the garrison of Grand Gulf, three brigades totalling some 7,500 men, in a series of strong defensive positions, intersected with deep ravines and covered with fallen timber and brushwood. Heavily outnumbered, they held on for most of the day, hoping that Loring's division, moving westwards along the battered railway-line through Newton, would come to their support. Particularly heavy casualties were suffered by the Boutetort Artillery, the only Virginia unit to take part in the Vicksburg campaign. Eventually, Bowen was forced back through Port Gibson and retired to his defences at Grand Gulf. Grant, who joined the battle with the two brigades of McPherson's Corps that had landed with him, was well satisfied by the performance of the troops. He was less so with that of McClernand who, he later claimed, had repeatedly asked for reinforcements when he was not under pressure and where, from the broken nature of the ground, there was no room for them to deploy.

The next morning the Union forces marched into Port Gibson, where the retreating Confederates had burnt the bridge over Bayou Pierre. The water-level was high and the stream fast, but Grant's army was by now well-practised in field engineering. Officers and men laboured together with little distinction of rank, and a floating bridge was speedily constructed with timber from nearby buildings and fences. While in the town, Grant read in a Southern newspaper of Grierson's exploits on the way to Baton Rouge, and appreciated his success in drawing troops away from the Mississippi.

On the Confederate side, Pemberton reported the battle at Port Gibson to Johnston and called for reinforcements. Johnston replied 'If General Grant's army lands on this side of the river, the safety of the Mississippi depends on beating it. For that object you should unite your whole force.' The message was repeated the next day. 'If Grant's army crosses, unite all your troops to beat him; success will give you back what was abandoned to win it.' He copied these messages to Richmond, adding that reinforcements on the scale asked for by Pemberton would mean giving up Tennessee. At this time neither general knew the full extent or exact location of Grant's invasion. Yet Vicksburg could not be left without a strong garrison, for, with the United States Navy controlling the rivers, Sherman might reappear as suddenly as he had gone. Much the same applied to Port Hudson which, with Vicksburg, had to be held as a vital connection between the Confederate States on either side of the river. If they fell because their defenders had been sent away to defeat Grant, it would not be as easy to recover them as Johnston implied. On the other hand, if Grant were victorious because Pemberton had not concentrated his forces, Vicksburg and Port Hudson, with their garrisons inside them, would be lost in any case.

Grant's wagon trains were still on the west side of the river. Remembering his experience of living off the land after losing his supply base at Holly Springs, he decided to do so again. The two days' 'hard-tack' in his men's packs would last five, especially if supplemented by fresh provisions of all kinds foraged from the countryside through which he intended to pass. The immediate transport requirement was for ammunition, since if there was to be hard fighting, his men could fire away in an hour all that they carried in their pouches. He gave orders for every draught animal and road vehicle in the neighbourhood of the bridge-head to be collected and used to carry ammunition. 'Quite a train was collected during the 30th, and a motley train it was,' he wrote in his Memoirs, '… fine carriages, loaded nearly to the top with boxes of ammunition that had been pitched in promiscuously, drawn by mules with plough-harness, straw collars, rope-lines, etc.; long-coupled wagons, with racks for carrying cotton-bales, drawn by oxen, and everything that could be found in the way of transportation on a plantation, either for use or pleasure.' As had been the case all the way from Milliken's Bend, no tentage was allowed for officers or men, and only one per company to shelter the rations, and one per formation headquarters for the paper-work essential to any modern army.

THE FALL OF GRAND GULF: 2 MAY 1863

Finding his position at Grand Gulf turned, Bowen retreated towards Vicksburg on 2 May after spiking his heavy guns and burying the lighter ones that he could not take with him. Loring met him at Hankinson's Ferry, a few miles up the Big Black from Grand Gulf, where they crossed over and marched to join Pemberton, then concentrating his forces between the river and the railway-line at Edwards. Porter arrived at Grand Gulf next day with *Benson*, *Carondelet*,

Lafayette, *Mound City* and *Pittsburg*, intending to renew his bombardment, but found the place deserted. After going ashore to survey the flotilla's handiwork, he began to write his dispatches to the Navy Department: 'We had a hard fight with these forts and it is with great pleasure I report that the Navy holds the key to Vicksburg.' Leaving orders for the abandoned guns and their ammunition to be taken on board by Lieutenant Commander Owen of *Louisville*, Porter prepared to get under way immediately for the Red River, where Banks was asking for support. 'I hear nothing of our army as yet,' he wrote. 'Was expecting to hear their guns as we advanced on the fort.' Shortly afterwards Grant rode into Grand Gulf on a borrowed horse with an escort of twenty cavalrymen. He went aboard *Benton* to confer with Porter and, having been in the field for nearly a month without his personal baggage, used the flagship's facilities to have a hot meal, take a bath and borrow a change of underwear from one of the naval officers.

Thus far, in accordance with Halleck's orders, Grant had planned to make Grand Gulf his supply base and to send McClernand's Corps south to co-operate with Banks in capturing Port Hudson, after which they would join forces and advance on Vicksburg. Banks, however, sent word to say that he was engaged in operations along the Red River and could not be at Port Hudson for another week, and then only with 15,000 men. Grant reckoned that, allowing for casualties and bridge guards along a three hundred mile line of march, this figure would have shrunk to 10,000 before Banks reached him. In the meanwhile the Confederates would have time to recover their balance and gather more reinforcements than could arrive with Banks. Justifying his decision on the grounds of urgency and the high state of his men's efficiency and morale, he later wrote: 'I determined to move independently of Banks, cut loose from my base, destroy the rebel force in rear of Vicksburg and invest or capture the city.' He reported his intentions accordingly, expecting that such a risky course of action would be disapproved, but knowing that it would take so long for his message to reach Washington and a reply to come back that it would be too late to stop him.

Grant accordingly ordered McClernand's XIII Corps to remain at Port Gibson while McPherson's XVII Corps held the line of the lower Big Black against any Confederate counter-offensive from Port Hudson. Sherman crossed the Mississippi to Grand Gulf with XV Corps and a column of wagons carrying three more days' hard rations, to reach Hankinson's Ferry on 8 May. From there he sent a message to Grant, who had already begun to move the other two corps eastwards, urging him to wait until more wagons came up and better roads had been built. 'This road', he said, 'will be jammed, sure as life.' In reply, Grant told him 'I do not calculate on supplying this army with full rations from Grand Gulf … what I do expect is to get up what rations of hard bread, coffee and salt we can, and make the country furnish the balance.'

In addition to the wagons that arrived with Sherman, another two hundred, laden with hard tack, coffee, sugar, salt and 100,000 pounds of salt meat were on their way from Young's Point. Foraging parties brought ample supplies of molasses, bacon, fresh meat and poultry, with vegetables and fruit for the men and hay for the animals. Grierson had reported much hardship and scarcity of provisions farther south, but this part of Mississippi seemed well able to feed Grant's 43,000 men. Only coffee and fresh bread were difficult to find. Plantation corn mills were set to work day and night along the line of advance, but could produce only enough for those units lucky enough to pass nearby.

On the Confederate side, Johnston, at Tullahoma, Tennessee, in the eastern part of his vast command area, received orders from Richmond on 9 May. He was to proceed at once to Mississippi 'and take chief command of the forces there, giving to those in the field, as far as practicable, the encouragement and benefit of your personal direction'. A large number of men taken prisoner at the Arkansas Post in the previous January had by this time been exchanged and were on their way to join Pemberton. Johnston was told to stop them and send them to Bragg in exchange for 3,000 good troops who were to go with him to Mississippi. He was also told he would find reinforcements coming from General Beauregard at Charleston, South Carolina. Still recovering from the effect of wounds received when commanding at Fair Oaks, Virginia, on 31 May 1862, he acknowledged the orders and replied 'I will go immediately, though unfit for field service.' Before leaving, he heard that Bragg's cavalry commander, the dashing Van Dorn, had been killed at Spring Hill, Tennessee, by Dr George B. Peters, for displaying excessive gallantry towards the doctor's wife. In agreement with Bragg, Johnston nominated Nathan Bedford Forrest to the vacant command.

Lieutenant General Nathan B. Forrest, who succeeded Earl Van Dorn as Bragg's cavalry commander.

During 10 and 11 May Grant continued to move north-eastwards, with McClernand holding the line of the Big Black on his left, Sherman in the centre, and McPherson passing through Utica, some twenty miles from Port Gibson, on the right. On 12 May, on the outskirts of Raymond, fifteen miles beyond Utica, McPherson encountered a brigade marching from Port Hudson under Brigadier General John Gregg. After a spirited attack and the loss of 515 casualties, the outnumbered Confederates were driven back and instead of joining Pemberton, retreated to Jackson, fifteen miles away. Raymond was then occupied and, in defiance of Grant's orders, plundered by the victorious Yankee soldiery. Gregg reached Jackson on 13 May, where he was joined by a brigade from Beauregard, the first of the reinforcements that Johnston had been promised. Johnston himself arrived during the night and learnt that Wirt Adams' cavalry had reported a Union corps of four divisions at Clinton, barely seven miles to the west, and thus between Johnston and Pemberton's main force at Edwards. He telegraphed the news to Richmond, ending with the emphasised words 'I am too late'.

THE BATTLE OF CHAMPION HILL (BAKER'S CREEK): 16 MAY 1863

Previous reports from Pemberton had led Johnston to believe that Grant's army was located south of Edwards. The troops reported at Clinton (actually two divisions of McClernand's Corps) must therefore, he supposed, have been detached from Grant's main force to prevent a Confederate concentration. He sent word to Pemberton during the night of 13 May to attack this presumed detachment with all his available forces, while the troops from Jackson marched to their support. His final words were 'Time is all-important'. At this time Johnston believed that by the following day, 14 May, further reinforcements from Beauregard and Port Hudson would have increased the size of his own force in Jackson to 12,000 men, and that Pemberton, with the entire garrison of Vicksburg in the field, could muster 23,000. He could reasonably expect that an immediate attack from both sides on a numerically inferior opponent would have every chance of success, and so allow the separated Confederate formations to join forces.

To ensure that his message reached Pemberton, Johnston sent copies by three different couriers and routes. Some months previously a man had been expelled with much publicity from Memphis by Major General Hurlbut for expressing anti-Union sentiments. He had made his way to the Confederate side, where he was taken into service and became one of the three couriers selected to take Johnston's message. In fact, the whole episode at Memphis had been a cleverly arranged charade. The individual in question was a Union agent and he rode straight to McPherson's lines, so that Grant read the message before the other two copies reached Pemberton.

Early on 14 May Johnston realised that two enemy Corps were marching on Jackson and that they would reach the city before his reinforcements arrived. His quartermaster general, anticipating this, had already prepared to move as much of his stores as he could. While two brigades under Gregg's command fought a delaying action, all the available wagons were loaded and moved five miles north of Jackson towards Canton. After a stout resistance the two brigades then followed, burning their own supply dumps and leaving behind seventeen guns and the Mississippi State capital. Having advanced through the continuing heavy rain, the muddied Union troops took possession of Jackson. There was what had become the usual outbreak of looting, although those terrified citizens who had not fled with Johnston were left at least personally unharmed. Grant moved into the city's finest hotel and occupied the bedroom in which Johnston had spent the previous night. Capturing Jackson had cost him 270 men killed, wounded and missing, against the Confederates' 845, including many taken prisoner.

On reading Johnston's intercepted message, Grant had ordered McClernand and McPherson to march rapidly towards Bolton, on the railway a few miles west of Clinton. Sherman was left in Jackson with two divisions to complete the destruction of everything of military value in the city. The railway lines and installations were destroyed and the arsenal, gun-foundry and carriage works were all burned, along with a factory (still in operation when Grant and Sherman entered it) making tent-cloth marked CSA. Confederate stragglers, runaway slaves and convicts released from the local gaol all took advantage of the collapse of civic authority to join in the looting, and several private residences and public buildings (including the gaol) were set on fire. Sherman followed Grant on 16 May, paroling his prisoners of war and leaving his wounded, for whom there was no transport, behind with their medical attendants. Soon afterwards Johnston re-occupied the city, amid cheers from the citizens and much waving of hand-kerchiefs by the ladies.

Grant's haste was based on the assumption that Pemberton would attack at Clinton, as ordered, and then go north to cross the Big Black and so return to reach Vicksburg ahead of him. In fact, Pemberton had established a strong and well-prepared position at Edwards and was confident of halting Grant there. Johnston's orders to assume the offensive required him not only to depart from this plan, but to abandon Vicksburg, which he had been ordered to hold at all costs by Jefferson Davis in person. Pemberton received the orders at his field headquarters in Bovina, west of the Big Black and half-way between Edwards and Vicksburg. He rode forward to join his army at Edwards and held a council of war with the generals there.

Pemberton's own view was that to advance directly on Clinton would be suicidal, as it would leave his southern flank open to attack, while the troops at Jackson would not be able to provide any effective co-operation. Moreover, the 'detachment' at Clinton might refuse to give battle and simply retreat, drawing him further away from Vicksburg while Grant's main force got between him and the city. Despite this, the majority of the council of war voted for moving on Clinton as ordered. Loring, supported by Stevenson, proposed a third option, marching from Edwards not to Clinton, but to Dillon's Plantation, about seven miles to the south, on the road from Grand Gulf. Accepting Pemberton's argument that they were not strong enough to attack Grant, they argued that by blocking his supply line there, they would force Grant to attack them.

In fact, there was no supply line to cut. The stores brought down from Milliken's Bend had all been out-loaded, and the last two hundred wagons from Grand Gulf reached Grant on the same day that Pemberton held his council of war. Unaware of this, Pemberton agreed to Loring's plan. As the indignant Johnston wrote later: 'Although averse to both opinions, General Pemberton adopted that of the minority of his council, and determined to execute a measure of which he disapproved, which his council of war opposed, and which was in violation of the orders of his commander.' The fact that the dispatch inform-ing Johnston of this was not written until eleven hours after his orders arrived and that it announced that no movement would begin until the next day, at a time when he had stressed the greatest need for urgency, struck Johnston, as he put it with commendable restraint, as 'very discouraging'.

Pemberton began his move south in the afternoon of 15 May, while Grant was marching west from Jackson. Baker's Creek, which lay between Edwards and Dillon's Plantation, was so swollen by heavy rain that bridges had been swept away and all the fords were impassable. This delayed his movements so that by first light on 16 May he was scarcely four miles away from his original position. Some of his men bivouacked on the estate of a wealthy planter, Sid Champion, who was away serving in a regiment of Mississippi Cavalry while his wife Matilda managed their plantation. From the grounds of the stately plantation house, the troops could see, on the road to Bolton, the camp-fires of Grant's 12th Division, commanded by the former Indiana lawyer, Brigadier General Alvin T. Hovey. In the early morning Pemberton received a message from Johnston informing him of the loss of Jackson and repeating the order to march on Clinton as the only practicable way to unite their two forces. He acknowledged and began to turn his wagon trains round, heading back the way they had come.

Already at Clinton, Grant received reports that Pemberton was moving eastwards with eighty regiments of infantry and ten batteries of artillery. While these troops waited for the wagons to clear the road, Wirt Adams' cavalry pickets were driven in by the advance of Hovey's Division. This formation, in McClernand's XIII Corps, had reached a cross-roads between Clinton and Raymond just ahead of John A. Logan's 3rd Division, part of McPherson's XVII Corps. In accordance with the conventions of the time, Hovey thus gained the right of way, notwithstanding a violent outburst of extremely profane language from the disappointed Logan, repeated when his Corps commander, McPherson, arrived shortly afterwards and declined to intervene.

Pemberton then decided to make a stand with his left (northerly) flank on Champion Hill, near his encampment of the previous night, from which a ridge extended about three miles to the south. On the east side of the ridge, facing the approaching Union troops, was a steep ravine. Beyond Pemberton's left, the ravine turned towards the west and joined Baker's Creek, from which the Confederate side would name the ensuing battle. The position, though lacking the defence works that had been constructed with such care at Edwards, was well-chosen. It was one of the highest points in the locality and artillery deployed on the upper slopes could cover all the approaching roads as well as the ground in front. The lower slopes were intersected by numerous gullies and covered with timber and underbrush. Pemberton had about 20,000 men in the field, consisting of three divisions commanded respectively by Stevenson, Bowen and Loring. He deployed these in line along the ridge, with Stevenson on his left, Bowen in the centre, and Loring on his right (southerly) flank.

There were several wagon-roads in the area, of which one, known as the Jackson Road, ran from Jackson to Vicksburg and marked the edge of Pemberton's left flank. At this point it turned south and went along the ridge for a mile or so before resuming its westerly course. It then descended a gentle slope for nearly another mile to cross a bridge over Baker's Creek. Another road, known as the Raymond Road, ran towards Vicksburg from Raymond and marked the edge of Pemberton's right flank. From there it continued westwards for about three miles before turning north to cross Baker's Creek some distance downstream of the bridge on the Jackson Road. A third road, branching off from one between Raymond and Bolton, climbed the ridge to join the Jackson Road. Hovey's Division, followed by McPherson's XVII Corps, approached from Bolton along the first of these roads, while the rest of McClernand's XIII Corps, with one of Sherman's divisions, moved from Raymond using the other two.

Grant was able to concentrate his own forces without enemy interference and, after some hours' skirmishing, the main combat began shortly before midday. Hovey attacked Stevenson's Division, on Pemberton's left, and drove it back amid heavy fighting. Logan arrived with his 3rd Division and, while one

A contemporary portrayal of the Battle of Champion Hill.

brigade joined the hard-pressed Hovey, the other two continued north-west-wards. This was to leave space for Crocker's 7th Division, coming up as fast as the muddy roads allowed. Two hours into the battle, Pemberton counter-attacked with Bowen's Division and recovered the guns and ground lost earlier. Captain Byers, adjutant of the 5th Iowa Infantry in Crocker's Division, recalled: 'We ran, and ran manfully … We tried to halt, and tried to form. It was no use. Again we ran, and harder, and farther, and faster. We passed over the very spot where, half an hour before, we left Grant leaning on his bay mare and smok-ing a cigar.'

Pemberton ordered Loring to send some of his troops to Stevenson's sup-port. Loring, however, reckoned that this would weaken his own position and allow McClernand, two miles in front of him, to advance and overwhelm the Confederate centre. In fact, this was what Grant had repeatedly ordered McClernand to do. Far from obeying, McClernand sent orders (promptly coun-termanded by Grant) for Hovey to move from his position in the battle line and rejoin his proper Corps. Grant, who had ridden to join Logan in the fighting on Pemberton's left, received urgent appeals from Hovey for reinforcements. With most of Sherman's Corps still miles away on the road from Jackson, and McClernand refusing to move, there were none to send. Not realising at the time that Logan had effectively turned the Confederates' flank and gained com-mand of their line of retreat to Baker's Creek, Grant ordered Logan and Crocker to move left to support Hovey. With their aid, Bowen's counter-attack, cruelly galled by flanking fire from McPherson's artillery, was finally halted and thrown back.

Then, in Pemberton's words, 'about four o'clock a part of Stevenson's division broke badly, and fell back in great disorder, but was partially rallied by the stren-uous exertions of myself and staff and put back under their own officers into the fight; but observing that large numbers of men were abandoning the field on Stevenson's left, deserting their comrades, who in this moment of greatest trial stood manfully at their posts, I rode up to General Stevenson, and, informing him that I had repeatedly ordered two brigades of General Loring's division to his assistance, and that I was momentarily expecting them, asked him whether he could hold his position. He replied that he could not; that he was fighting from sixty to eighty thousand men.' Pemberton then rode off to find Loring and, on meeting one of the brigades that had been sent for, detached one regiment to reinforce Bowen and ordered the rest to join Stevenson. Of Loring himself, despite several members of Pemberton's staff being sent to find him, there seemed no trace. In fact he had left one of his two remaining brigades, com-manded by Brigadier General Lloyd Tilghman, to hold the Raymond Road, and moved with the other along a country road to support Stevenson on the left of the Confederate line.

For the Confederates, the day was lost. Bowen reported in person that he could no longer hold his position. Colonel Edward Goodwin, commanding the

35th Alabama Infantry in Loring's division, recalled: 'At this time our friends gave way and came rushing to the rear panic-stricken … The Colours of three regiments passed through … We collared them, begged them, and abused them in vain.' With his outnumbered line collapsing, Pemberton was forced to retreat. Later, he was inclined to blame Loring for disregarding orders, though he himself had disregarded those from Johnston. The two divisions that Pemberton had left behind to guard Vicksburg, despite having been told by Johnston to concentrate all his forces, would have given him a reserve with which he might at least have held the ridge until nightfall. From Pemberton's own account, however, it is clear that, faced by a superior force (Grant had seven divisions present at Champion Hill and the other five coming up in support), he always intended to return to Vicksburg. On the Union side, Grant blamed McClernand for a similar refusal to obey orders. If his XIII Corps had come forward as directed, there would have been no need to send Logan back to Hovey's aid and so leave the way open for Pemberton's retreat.

During the morning, Pemberton's engineers had constructed a bridge over Baker's Creek where it was crossed by the Raymond Road. At the same time the water level had fallen, allowing the ford there to be used, so that it was by this road that Pemberton decided to withdraw. Loring, rejoined by his detached brigades, formed the rearguard. Tilghman, encouraging his men to stand firm and cover the retreat, was killed by shell-fire, in the bloodiest and most bitterly contested battle of the entire Vicksburg campaign. On the Union side, casualties amounted to 410 killed, 1,844 wounded and 187 missing, most of them from Hovey's Division, which suffered more than 30 per cent casualties. Hovey afterwards wrote that he never saw such fighting. 'I cannot think of this bloody hill without sadness and pride. It was, after the conflict, literally the hill of death.' The Confederates lost 381 killed, 1,800 wounded and 1,670 missing, together with twenty-seven guns. Most of the wounded and missing became prisoners of war.

Wounded men of both sides were treated by Union medical officers who came forward to set up field hospitals in abandoned houses, or take over similar dressing-stations left by the Confederates. With no means but amputation to prevent the onset of gangrene in shattered limbs, the surgeons used what primitive anaesthetics and antiseptics they had, but relied mostly on speed to minimise suffering. The effect of shock and loss of blood meant that recovery was problematic and survival often merely a matter of days. Grant's staff, still without tentage, set up his headquarters in the porch of a house that had been turned into a Confederate field hospital and was full of wounded enemy soldiers. In his Memoirs, he reflected on the paradox of warfare among civilised men. 'While a battle is raging, one can see his enemy mowed down by the thousand, or the ten thousand, with great composure; but after the battle these scenes are distressing, and one is naturally disposed to do as much to alleviate the suffering of an enemy as a friend.'

THE BATTLE OF THE BIG BLACK: 17 MAY 1863

Knowing that Pemberton was under orders from Johnston to attempt a combination of their two forces, Grant pressed closely on the retreating Confederates. While admitting that, if Pemberton had marched north-east to join Johnston, Vicksburg might have been easily taken, Grant believed that was the more sound military move. With no more ammunition than what he carried with him, and his ability to live off the country reduced if he had to face strong opposition, it was essential for Grant to keep the two Confederate forces apart. Hovey's badly depleted division was ordered to stay where it was. McPherson's Corps refilled its pouches and then, leaving one brigade with the wounded, moved forward in the pursuit. Stevenson reached Baker's Creek by the Raymond Road at sunset. He found it already under long-range fire from a field battery of Carr's 14th Division which had crossed upstream by the Jackson Road. He sent word to Loring that he would hold the Raymond Road crossing for him, but Loring, his division already cut off, moved away southwards. After crossing Baker's Creek, Stevenson continued along the road through Edwards and over the Big Black to join Pemberton at Bovina during the night.

Pemberton decided to hold the Jackson Road at the crossing of the Big Black so that Loring, whom he expected to arrive with the enemy in close pursuit, could make a safe passage. The position was a strong one, with the river meandering in a characteristic horse-shoe shape, the open side towards the east. About three-quarters of a mile before reaching the river, the Jackson Road crossed a long shallow bayou. To the north, the bayou emptied directly into the Big Black, while to the south it ended in a thicket that stretched almost to the river-bank farther downstream. This bayou became the basis of the Confederate line. The surrounding area was mostly open, cultivated fields, interspersed with blocks of woodland, though at the northern end, where the bayou approached the river, there was a swampy depression. The bayou was a significant obstacle, strengthened by the trees that grew in it being felled with their branches towards the enemy and by a breastwork of cotton bales covered with earth. It was covered by a mile-long line of rifle-pits interspersed with gun platforms. The Jackson Road ran alongside the railway towards Vicksburg and crossed the river by Smith's Ferry, the railway being carried across on a trestle bridge. This bridge had been floored to allow it to be used by artillery and wagons, and another bridge had been made beside it by mooring the decommissioned steamer *Dot* fore and aft athwart the river.

Bowen was left with about 4,000 men and twenty guns, all that could be deployed in the ground available, to hold the bridgehead long enough for Loring to arrive and cross the river. The left of the line was manned by one brigade from Bowen's original division and the right by another. The centre was given to a fresh brigade that had not been engaged at Champion Hill and was assumed by Pemberton to have a high morale. The weakness of the position, like that of all bridgeheads, was that its defenders had a major obstacle, in this case the Big Black, in its rear. Nevertheless, it needed to be held only long enough for Loring's division to pass through. Loring could then stand on the bluffs on the Vicksburg side of the river and cover Bowen's withdrawal to join him. In fact, Loring had continued southwards during the night, looking for a way round Grant's army. At dawn, while Pemberton held the crossing of the Big Black for him, he turned away towards Crystal Springs, some twenty miles to the south-east. From there he marched north-east towards Jackson, where he joined Johnston some days later.

It was therefore not Loring's division that the Confederate outposts saw approaching in the early morning of 17 May, but the leading elements of McClernand's Corps, on the move since first light in response to Grant's urgent orders. Carr's 14th Division was the first to arrive and deployed with its left, or southern, flank on the Jackson Road and its right extending north to the Big

Sherman's pontoon bridge over the Big Black River at Bridgeport. Sherman had the only pontoon train in the army, and this was the first of the Union bridges over the river.

William Wing Loring (1818–1886) later fought abroad in the army of the Khedive of Egypt and fought in the Abyssinian War of 1875–9.

Black, upstream of the confluence with the bayou. Osterhaus' 9th Division arrived next and deployed across the Jackson Road about half a mile in front of the Confederate line, followed by Andrew J. Smith's 10th Division, which joined Osterhaus' left. The action began with an artillery duel, accompanied by lively skirmishing-fire by the opposing infantry along most of the front. One of Carr's brigades worked its way along the river to reach the swampy depression on the north side of the battlefield, while another massed in an adjacent block of woodland. Both these features concealed them from the Confederate defenders, who were then surprised by a sudden charge that swept across their left front to strike the brigade holding the centre.

As Pemberton reported: 'The enemy … advanced at a run, with loud cheers. Our troops in their front did not wait to receive them, but broke and fled precipitately. One portion of the line being broken, it very soon became a matter of *sauve qui peut* … A strong position, with an ample force of infantry to hold it, was shamefully abandoned, almost without resistance. The troops occupying the centre did not do their duty. With an almost impassable bayou between them and the enemy, they fled before the enemy reached that obstacle.' In accordance with standard procedure, his artillerymen had established their wagon lines well behind the guns, so that the horses and reserve ammunition limbers would be away from hostile fire. On this occasion, the position chosen was so far to the rear that, when the infantry line gave way, the gun-teams could not reach the batteries before they were overrun and most of the guns were lost. When the Confederate centre collapsed, the two flank brigades joined the rout, and fell back in disorder towards the bridges. Men who had fought bravely the previous day found their well of courage drained by the combination of defeat, combat fatigue and two nights' sleep deprivation. The few guns that had not been unlimbered crossed to safety, as did most of the infantry. Many men tried to escape by swimming across the river, though it was still swollen by the recent rain, and a number were drowned in the attempt. Many more, either unable to swim or prevented from reaching the river by enemy fire, remained in the rifle pits until they were captured. The Union losses amounted to 30 killed, 237 wounded and three missing. The Confederates lost 1,751 men taken prisoner, but, from their rapid retreat, suffered few other casualties, most of them men who drowned while trying to cross the river.

Pemberton did his best to rally his troops by his personal presence, but the general and his soldiers had lost confidence in each other at this time. The best he could do was to add the few guns that escaped from the bridgehead to those already in position on the bluffs on the Vicksburg bank, while two brigades, recalled from Bovina, covered the retreat. This delayed McClernand's advance long enough for the railway bridge and *Dot* to be set on fire, a significant achievement, for, as Grant wrote: 'But for the successful and completed destruction of the bridge, I have but little doubt that we should have followed the enemy so closely as to prevent his occupying his defences around Vicksburg.' Pemberton decided that it was impossible to remain on the Big Black. With no sign of Loring, he had lost a third of his field army and could be easily outflanked if Grant crossed the river upstream at Bridgeport, or downstream at Baldwin's Ferry. The troops that remained with him seemed completely demoralised and their fighting efficiency was further weakened by the absence of large numbers of men who had become separated from their regiments during the rout and were straggling back towards Vicksburg. Many had cast away their weapons and knapsacks as they ran. He therefore ordered a retreat to the Vicksburg defence perimeter, seven miles away, leaving Stevenson to command the rearguard while he himself rode ahead to begin re-organising his army.

In his dispatches to Richmond, Pemberton later reported that the retreat was executed without haste and in good order. Citizens in Vicksburg did not see it in the same light. Emma Balfour, the 45-year-old wife of a prosperous physician, whose house was next to the one in which Pemberton established his headquarters, wrote: 'I hope never to witness again such a scene as the return of our routed army. From 12 o'clock until late in the night the streets and roads were jammed with wagons, cannons, horses, men … Nothing like order prevailed, of course.' The confusion was made worse by droves of cattle, pigs and sheep, brought in on Pemberton's orders from the farms along the road to add to the provisions of a garrison about to withstand a siege. Outside the city, some ladies told the dispirited men passing their gates 'Why don't you stand your ground? Shame on you all!' One soldier replied that they had never run before, but had been unable to stand alone when the rest of the army broke. Others blamed Pemberton ('Old Pem'), for their defeat. Many citizens took pity on the exhausted troops, and gave them water, food and a place to rest. Several clergymen and physicians were reported as having gone out to minister to the wounded and dying. A visiting Methodist preacher told the ladies of his congregation (it was a Sunday, so all were in church) to go home and prepare lint and bandages.

On the Union side, Sherman had marched westwards out of Jackson with his two divisions at about noon on 16 May and reached Bolton, about twelve miles away, before dawn the next day. Too far away to reach the battle of Champion Hill, he was ordered north to cross the Big Black at Bridgeport, where Blair's 2nd Division would rejoin his Corps. Sherman arrived there at about noon on 17 May and found Blair's pontoon train waiting for him. The few Confederate defenders entrenched on the far bank were shelled into surrender and, after the pontoon bridge had been built, Blair's Division and Steele's 1st Division, went over during the night. Tuttle's 3rd Division, played across by its bands, followed early the next morning. Grant, smoking his usual cigar, joined Sherman and sat with him on a log to watch the regiments go by. 'The whole scene was lit up by fires of pitch-pine,' Sherman later wrote '… the bridge swayed to and fro under the passing feet, and made a fine war picture.'

A short distance downstream, at the little settlement of Amsterdam, McPherson's Corps used local materials to build three bridges. One, constructed by Lieutenant Hains of the Engineers, was a raft of floating timbers. Another, under Brigadier General Thomas E. G. Ransom, was made by felling trees from opposite banks of the river, so that their branches connected across the stream and supported decking laid over them. The third, built under the personal supervision of McPherson, used cotton bales as pontoons. His troops completed their passage of the Big Black in the morning of 18 May and the whole army then pressed on towards Vicksburg.

Pemberton had already decided that the defences on the Chickasaw Bluffs were too far away from Vicksburg to be tenable against a landward attack and ordered their garrisons back into the city. Boats laden with corn were sent up the Yazoo, as there were no wagons to bring their cargo into Vicksburg. Two companies were left behind with orders to destroy everything that could not be moved and to make a show of force until the approach of the enemy obliged them to retire. Grant and Sherman, riding with the forward skirmish-line to the positions where Sherman had been defeated the previous December, found themselves under fire as the companies made their way back into Vicksburg. Grant's cavalry rode into the once impregnable defence-works to find them almost deserted and the heavy guns spiked. Below Vicksburg, the batteries at Warrenton were also abandoned and their lighter guns redeployed within the city's defences. Wirt Adams and the cavalry, use-less mouths in a siege, were ordered to hang upon Grant's flank and rear and disrupt his supplies.

From Grand Gulf, Porter took his gunboats down to the Red River, where he met *Albatross*, *Estrella* and *Arizona* returning from their attack on Fort De Russey. While Farragut and *Hartford* returned to New Orleans, Porter took over command on the Mississippi. Going up to renew the attack on De Russey, he found it deserted and then steamed on to reach Alexandria a day ahead of Banks's advancing army. The Confederates had lightened their own river-boats and taken them hundreds of miles further up the Red River, so Porter, with the water level falling, returned to Grand Gulf. Leaving part of the flotilla there, he went up-river to re-establish contact with the gunboats at Milliken's Bend on 15 May. Three days later, the sound of gunfire behind Vicksburg and the sight of Union artillery moving into position at Snyder's Bluff indicated that Grant had reached the Yazoo. Porter at once sent gunboats to join the troops there and, with the Yazoo cleared, transport steamers came from Milliken's Bend to replenish Grant's dwindling ammunition and bring his men the fresh bread and coffee that they craved.

The risks Grant had taken in first moving down the Mississippi, with only a single waterlogged road between his base and his army, then crossing the river into enemy territory and finally advancing with no supply-line at all until he could defeat his opponents and reach the Yazoo, had proved justified. Within twenty days of crossing the river at Bruinsburg his army had fought and won five battles, captured six thousand prisoners and eighty-eight pieces of artillery, marched an average of 180 miles on five days' issue of rations and opened the four hundred miles of river between Vicksburg and Port Hudson for losses of 695 killed, 3,425 wounded, and 259 missing. Had the Confederates been able to combine their forces against him, the issue might have been in doubt. As Grant put it: 'We were fortunate, to say the least, in meeting them in detail.' Good fortune, however, is an essential attribute of successful commanders, and Grant's men had come to believe that their general's star was in the ascendant.

Fort Castle, one of the strongest of Vicksburg's defensive points. Overlooking the river, it housed the powerful gun known as 'Whistling Dick' illustrated on page 106.

SIEGE WARFARE

THE DEFENCES

The landward defences of Vicksburg had been planned and constructed during the previous autumn by Major Samuel H. Lockett, Pemberton's chief engineer. The major fortifications consisted of earthworks spaced at roughly 200-yard intervals, each mounting artillery emplacements, strengthened with heavy timbers and protected by formidable ditches filled with stakes, wire entanglements and other obstacles. These works were connected by lines of entrenchments and rifle-pits sited to cover the intervening ravines and command the routes into the city. In some places however, the lines were protected only by loose palings and in others there were areas of dead ground where defensive fire could not be brought to bear. With the heaviest guns sited against the gunboats, those on the landward side were field pieces, mostly mounted *en barbette*, high up in raised emplacements, from which they fired over the parapets rather than through them. This gave them good fields of fire, but left them vulnerable to counter-battery fire and enemy sharpshooters.

The whole position took the shape of an irregular oblong, with the two shorter sides, each about a mile and a half long, on the north and south respectively. The two longer sides, with the western one running along the bank of the Mississippi, each stretched over some seven miles. On the north, the ground rose to two hundred feet above the river. On the south, it was lower and under cultivation, but the defence was aided by many gullies and watercourses. Outside the lines, houses that had been built in happier times as country retreats were burnt down, to deny them to the approaching enemy and to clear the defenders' fields of fire.

Inside its defences, the city that had for so long defied the river gunboats now stood ready for Grant. Of the four divisions forming the garrison, two, commanded respectively by Major Generals John H. Forney and Martin L. Smith, had not been involved in the combats at Champion Hill and the Big Black. The other two, those of Stevenson and Bowen, had rallied on reaching the defences, while regimental bands boosted morale with rousing airs. Men without weapons were re-armed from the ordnance parks and stragglers rejoined their colours. On the way back from the Big Black, a dispirited Pemberton had told Lockett that it was thirty years to the day since he had begun his career as a soldier and it had all ended in defeat and disgrace. Now, like his men, he regained his determination. He calculated that he could muster 31,000 against Grant's estimated 45,000 (actually less than 43,000), but would be fighting behind strong defences, with a hundred and two guns of various nature in position and enough food and ammunition to hold out for weeks, while Johnston, a mere fifty miles away, marched to his relief. There was sufficient lead and paper to keep up the supply of cartridges, and the only shortage was of percussion caps for the muskets. Even these, given their small bulk, could be carried by the thousand in the saddle-bags of couriers who were still able to reach the city.

Pemberton reported to Johnston the defeat at the Big Black, the retreat into Vicksburg and the abandonment of the city's outlying defences along the Yazoo. At noon on 18 May he was astonished to receive a reply reading: 'If Haines' Bluff is untenable, Vicksburg is of no value, and cannot be held. If therefore, you are invested in Vicksburg, you must ultimately surrender. Under such circum-stances, instead of losing both troops and place, we must, if possible save the troops. If it is not too late, evacuate Vicksburg and its dependencies, and march to the north-east.' Months later, in his report to Richmond, Pemberton was moved to use an exclamation mark. 'The evacuation of Vicksburg! It meant the loss of the valuable stores and munitions of war collected for its defense, the fall of Port Hudson, the surrender of the Mississippi River and the severance of the Confederacy. These were mighty interests, which, had I deemed the evacuation practicable in the sense in which I interpreted General Johnston's instructions, might well have made me hesitate to execute them.' Knowing the importance placed on Vicksburg by public opinion throughout the South, he immediately convened a council of war to discuss the practicability of Johnston's orders.

All agreed that it would be impossible to take the army out of Vicksburg in any state to be of any further use to the Confederacy. In effect, it could stay and fight, or break out and break up. It could not break out and fight as Johnston wished. Pemberton therefore replied that he had decided to hold Vicksburg as long as possible 'with the firm hope that the Government may yet be able to assist me in keeping this obstruction to the enemy's free navigation of the Mississippi River. I still conceive it to be the most important point in the Confederacy.' This may have been a hint that Pemberton would appeal to Jefferson Davis, who had repeatedly stressed the importance of holding Vicksburg. Johnston was obliged to accept that Pemberton's army was not in a condition to take the field, and sent an answer saying, rather vaguely 'I am trying to gather a force which may attempt to relieve you. Hold out.'

Part of the Confederate defensive works at Vicksburg.

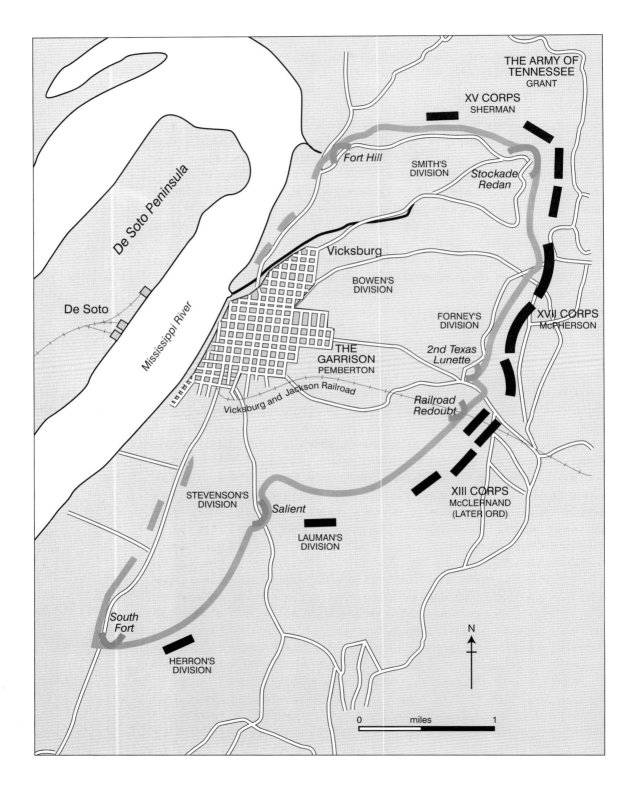

THE ARMY OF
TENNESSEE
GRANT

XV CORPS
SHERMAN

Fort Hill

SMITH'S
DIVISION

Stockade
Redan

Vicksburg

BOWEN'S
DIVISION

FORNEY'S
DIVISION

XVII CORPS
McPHERSON

De Soto Peninsula

De Soto

Mississippi River

THE
GARRISON
PEMBERTON

2nd Texas
Lunette

Vicksburg and Jackson Railroad

Railroad
Redoubt

STEVENSON'S
DIVISION

Salient

XIII CORPS
McCLERNAND
(LATER ORD)

LAUMAN'S
DIVISION

N

South
Fort

HERRON'S
DIVISION

0   miles   1

On 19 May, the day after reaching Pemberton's defence lines, Grant decided to carry them by storm. This was standard military practice when a defeated army had been driven within the walls of a fortress. It was held that, in such circumstances, the defenders would still be demoralised and would not have had the chance to re-organise. The attackers, on the other hand, would have all the impetus gained from their previous success. Less than nine years earlier, the failure of the British and French commanders to follow up their defeat of the Russians at the Alma by making an immediate attack on Sevastopol had condemned their men to the horrors of a lengthy siege in the bitter cold of a Crimean winter. Grant was concerned to spare his men comparable hardships in the intense heat of a Mississippi summer. He was, moreover, as confident as they were that victory lay within their grasp and his views were shared by his three Corps commanders. His engineers, after fulfilling their first duty when any attack on a fortification was at hand, that of surveying the enemy's defences, were more cautious and warned that many of the strong-points would be impassable. Down on the river, with his flag in the converted riverboat *Black Hawk*, Porter wrote to Hurlbut at Memphis to say that, although he had no authority to say as much, Grant should be sent reinforcements without delay, as 'he will have the hardest fight ever seen during the war'. His mortar-boats, together with two heavy guns on the De Soto Peninsula, had maintained a periodic fire on the city, testing the defences and registering the ranges. Now they began a continuous heavy bombardment.

THE FIRST ASSAULT: 19 MAY 1863

The attack began at 2 p.m. on 19 May, when Blair's Division moved forward against the Stockade Redan, in the north-east corner of the Confederate position. Heavy fire from strong defences stoutly manned by Martin L. Smith's Division, forced the leading brigade to halt and reform three times before crossing the broken, obstacle-filled ground to launch the assault. The 13th United States Infantry, Grant's only regular foot soldiers, stormed forward to within twenty-five yards of the Redan, but were then forced to go to ground. With Confederate marksmen carefully picking off its key personnel, the regiment lost many of its officers and five colour-bearers in succession, with a total casualty rate of 43 per cent. Its regimental colour was hit fifty-five times, and afterwards, by Sherman's orders, bore the battle honour 'First at Vicksburg'. In the next brigade, the 55th Illinois Infantry ran out of ammunition. A 14-year-old drummer, whose standard duties included bringing ammunition to the firing line, volunteered to run to neighbouring units for more. With the new supply line from the Yazoo not yet open, none had rounds to spare. Looking for a replenishment point, the drummer was stopped by Sherman himself, who asked 'What is the matter, my boy?' Hearing the story and noticing that he was bleeding from a leg wound, Sherman ordered him to the rear, but Drummer Orion P. Howe insisted that his first duty was to collect the ammunition for his regiment. It was only after Sherman, with enemy artillery fire falling around them, promised to resolve the re-supply problem in person that Howe limped off for medical attention. Thirty-three years later he received the Congressional Medal of Honor, one of the three awarded for feats performed that day.

McPherson, on Sherman's left, and McClernand, at the southern end of the attack, came into action later, but with little more success. After nightfall, those units that had been trapped in front of the Confederate works escaped back to their own lines. Elsewhere, though the works had not been stormed, areas of ground close to them had been gained and Grant, facing the first repulse of his campaign, consoled himself with the thought that these would be useful for his next attack. He had nevertheless lost 157 men killed, 777 wounded, and eight missing.

Along with most of his men, Grant still believed that the city could be taken by storm and that, although the first rush had failed, a more carefully prepared assault would succeed. Like Pemberton, he believed that Johnston was nearby, with a reinforced army, and would soon be moving to Vicksburg's relief. He therefore aimed to capture the city before relief arrived, after which he could turn and defeat Johnston without calling on other theatres for the troops that would be needed for a lengthy siege. He also took into account the spirit of his men, who, at least in his later view, would not willingly have endured the hardships of a siege while they thought that Vicksburg might have fallen to a *coup de main*. Certainly, most were confident of a speedy victory. Some even regretted that, having lived in the field for a month, they would not have smart uniforms in which to impress the Southern belles.

By this time supplies of ammunition, fresh bread, tents and cooking equipment were beginning to pass down the wagon road from the Yazoo. 'I remember', wrote Grant, 'that in passing around to the left of the line on the 21st, a soldier, recognizing me, said in a rather low voice, yet so that I heard him, "Hard Tack". In a moment the cry was taken up all along the line "Hard Tack! Hard Tack!" I told the men nearest to me that we had been engaged ever since the arrival of the troops in building a road over which to supply them with everything they needed. The cry instantly changed to cheers. By the night of the 21st all the troops had full rations issued to them. The bread and coffee were highly appreciated.' Nevertheless, men of the 20th Ohio Infantry, who had been in the thick of the fighting at Champion Hill, knew that a victory would not be without cost. Before moving off to their assault positions, many took the precaution of leaving personal items and keepsakes for their loved ones in the care of the regimental cooks, whose duties placed them among those left out of battle.

THE SECOND ASSAULT: 22 MAY 1863

Early on 22 May the Union forces began a heavy bombardment both from the land and the river. The mortar-boats ranged on targets within the city and gunboats came out to duel with the water batteries, though an intercepted dispatch from Grant to one of the naval commanders meant that the Confederates were ready for them. The landward attack began at 10 a.m., the three Corps commanders having set their watches by Grant's to ensure that all moved at the same time. As previously, Sherman's main assault was against Stockade Redan, held by Martin L. Smith's Division. At the head was the 150-strong Forlorn Hope, a corruption of the Dutch for 'Lost Party', applied to the leading storm-troopers since the days of siege warfare in the Spanish Netherlands. These men, the bravest of the brave and by convention all volunteers, were drawn from fifteen different regiments. Despite the aid of a portable wooden bridge (made from the timber of a nearby house in which Grant had been trying to sleep), they found that the defensive ditch, six feet deep and eight feet wide, was impassable. The stormers, led by Captain Richard H. Wood, 97th Illinois Infantry, could jump down into it, but not climb the steep bank beyond to reach the parapet seventeen feet above them. The defenders, having made their own preparations in the intervening two days, used hand-grenades against troops taking shelter in the ditch. Most exploded among their targets, though a few, with their fuses still burning, were picked up and thrown back, or knocked away by men using their bayonets like baseball bats. All along the line, the Confederate defenders, under orders to conserve ammunition, held their fire until the assaulting troops appeared out of the battle smoke, and then shot them down at close range. After nearly two hours' bitter fighting, Sherman's attack came to a halt.

On Sherman's left flank, McPherson found the Confederate defences, held by Forney's Division, equally impenetrable. Despite heavy artillery and musketry fire, a number of colour-bearers reached the parapets of the Great and 3rd Louisiana Redans, but few of the attackers, rushing desperately forward as their disordered lines grew steadily thinner, survived to follow them. Those that did were pulled over the parapets and captured. South of the railway, McClernand attacked the lines held by Stevenson's Division and initially made good progress. The 22nd Iowa Infantry, in Carr's Division, entered the Railroad Redoubt through a breach in its salient angle and Union battle flags were planted on neighbouring Confederate works. Nevertheless, these successes were achieved at the cost of heavy casualties and after an hour McClernand sent a message to Grant asking for reinforcements to exploit his gains.

Sylvanus Cadwallader, a newspaper correspondent representing the Chicago *Times*, watched McClernand's attack and believed it was failing. Later, he repeated the perennial complaint of infantrymen that they had suffered casualties from their own artillery fire, in this case as an alleged consequence of badly manufactured fuses in their Hotchkiss shells. Nevertheless, the gunners were not to be outdone in courage by their infantry comrades, as was demonstrated when Captain Patrick H. White and a detachment of the Chicago Mercantile Battery man-handled their gun up to the enemy works and fired it through one of the embrasures.

Grant, who thought McClernand was over-ready to ask for reinforcements, sent none and after an hour and a half's fighting decided that the operation was a failure. While he was in conference with Sherman, another message arrived from McClernand, reporting that his men were in part possession of two forts and should be supported by a vigorous attack all along the line. Grant, nearly two miles away, declared that he could see the position as well as McClernand and did not believe that the report was reliable. In fact, it was accurate as far as it went, for McClernand was indeed in part possession of the forts, and, as he said in his subsequent dispatches, wanted reinforcements to expand the lodgement his men had made. Sherman 'not dreaming that a Major General would at such a critical moment make a mere buncombe communication', as he afterwards wrote, persuaded Grant that an official message from a Corps commander could not be disregarded. Grant accordingly ordered Sherman and McPherson to attack during the afternoon, with Quinby's 7th Division being sent from McPherson to reinforce McClernand. After a difficult approach march, this division reached McClernand at dusk and was immediately committed to an assault. It proved another costly failure, and even the Railway Redoubt was lost to a counter-attack by the Texas Legion. By nightfall the Army of the Tennessee was

Battery Sherman, on the Jackson Road, before Vicksburg, one of 89 battery positions constructed by Grant's army.

back at its start-line, having suffered 502 killed, including one general officer; 2,550 wounded and 147 missing, against Confederate losses of less than 500. Vicksburg, the Gibraltar of the Mississippi, was still unconquered.

For all the valour of his men, Grant had suffered a defeat. It was, he later said, one of the two assaults during the war that he wished he had never ordered. Backed by Sherman, he was inclined to blame McClernand, whom neither of them liked or respected, for giving a false report. Sherman, indeed, argued that the two forts of which McClernand had spoken were mere lunettes, little more than breastworks, open at the back, and commanded by more formidable fortifications behind them. Two days later, writing to Halleck, Grant complained that he had been misled by McClernand and blamed him for the losses suffered during the afternoon attacks, adding 'He is entirely unfit for the position of corps commander, both on the march and on the battlefield.' Nevertheless, Grant himself, as army commander, could be blamed for not making a personal reconnaissance before renewing the attack, especially if he distrusted McClernand's judgement. Like the generals of the First World War that would come half a century later, Grant may have fallen prey to the belief that, despite the repulse of his first attack, the enemy had been weakened by it and that one last push would break the defenders' line. When that push failed, he decided that it would indeed be the last, and immediately opened the approaches to reduce Vicksburg by siege.

More than thirty years later, Congressional Medals of Honor were awarded to the survivors of those who distinguished themselves on 22 May. Among them were Captain Wood, 97th Illinois Infantry; Captain Nicholas Geshwind, 16th Illinois Infantry; First Lieutenant John H. Frisler, 55th Illinois Infantry; and First Lieutenant George H. Stockman, 6th Missouri Infantry, with eight sergeants, eleven corporals and fifty-six private soldiers who fought under these officers as members of the Forlorn Hope; Captain White and the six artillerymen of the Chicago Mercantile Battery who manhandled their gun up to the enemy embrasure; Corporal Isaac H. Carmin, 48th Ohio Infantry, who saved his regimental colour and threw away a shell that, with its fuse still burning, had landed among his comrades in the ditch, and five others who carried their regimental colours during the assaults of the day.

After the assault, the Union dead and wounded lay out in the sun where they had fallen. Accounts vary in explaining the delay in performing the elementary duty of collecting them. One version is that Grant asked for the usual truce, only for it to be denied by Pemberton on the grounds that the action was still in progress. Another is that, despite his humanitarian inclinations, Grant did not wish to show weakness by seeking a favour from the enemy. Eventually, with the obnoxious sickly-sweet smell of death reaching Vicksburg from the battlefield two miles away, and everyone's health put at risk by the decomposing, fly-blown corpses, Pemberton opened the question on 25 May. '… in the name of humanity,' he wrote to Grant, 'I have the honor to propose a cessation of hostilities for two hours and a half, that you may be enabled to remove your dead and dying men.' Grant agreed to the proposal and ordered a temporary armistice while both sides came out to undertake the necessary tasks.

Even before the action of 22 May, the positions of the two armies had been close enough for the soldiers to shout to one another across the lines. Two brigades of troops from Missouri, one in each army, found themselves facing one other, and the Union soldiers responded to Confederate enquiries about the friends and families they had left behind. Several men discovered mutual acquaintances and one, serving in the 3rd Louisiana Infantry, was invited across the lines and hospitably entertained before returning to his unit. In the same regiment, two men found that they had brothers serving in the enemy unit facing them. Some Confederate soldiers invited the Yankees to lend them some coffee to have with their supper, promising to pay it back as soon as Johnston arrived. Their drollery received the reply that Grant would be dining with them inside Vicksburg on the morrow.

During the truce, fraternisation spread. Sherman himself spotted a Confederate officer (actually Major Samuel H. Lockett, Pemberton's chief engineer, who had gone out to examine his works from the enemy side) and courteously sent an orderly to invite him over. He had, he explained, some mail for members of the garrison from some of their Northern friends and wished to deliver it before it became too old. Lockett was gratified to hear Sherman comment favourably on the advantage that had been taken of a naturally strong position (unaware that Lockett was the designer) but replied that the mail would indeed become old if it waited for Sherman to deliver it in person. Not to be outdone, Sherman answered that though a siege was a slow way of delivering mail, it was a sure one, and he was determined that the letters should get through sooner or later.

On both sides, there were expressions of regret that events had made enemies of former friends. Some Union troops, well supplied by the river steamers, shared their food and drink with their enemies. A few Southerners decided not to return to their lines, but most stood stoutly by the justice of their Cause. Confederate Brigadier General Stephen D. Lee told Mrs Balfour that he for one had declined the offer of a glass from a Union general and had spoken his mind on the naval bombardment of women, children and sick inside the city. The Northerners remained confident of continued victory, though some were reported as saying that they would be happy to go home and leave the South alone. At 9 p.m. the truce ended and the snipers, mortar-men and gunners resumed their activities. While outlying pickets continued to chat across the lines, their comrades took up picks and shovels to strengthen their trenches and extend their works.

THE SIEGE CAMPAIGN

Determined to waste no more lives, Grant began a siege. All the scientific techniques and procedures that military engineers had developed since the emergence of modern fortress design three centuries earlier now came into play, with moves as formal and prescribed as the figures and rituals of a stately dance. His troops started to dig trenches in a series of carefully calculated zig-zag lines, the angles becoming increasingly sharp as they approached the enemy works, to stop the garrison gunners firing down them. Around the city, he built a line of circumvallation to keep the garrison in, and a line of contravallation to keep would-be relievers out.

Grant had already been strengthened by the arrival at Snyder's Bluff on 20 May of XVI Corps' 4th Division from Memphis, under Jacob G. Lauman. This moved into the line on the left of McClernand's XIII Corps on 24 May. Other formations followed, as Halleck, reinforcing success, also sent more troops. The investment was completed on 13 June, when an unattached division under Major General Francis J. Herron arrived from Missouri and closed the gap between Lauman's Division and the river south of Vicksburg. When Major General Parke arrived from the Ohio with his IX Corps shortly afterwards, the besieging force reached a total of some 75,000 men and 220 guns. Of the gunners, only the regulars of the 1st US Artillery, with their six 32-pdrs, were trained siege artillerymen. There were no other siege guns in the whole of the western theatre, but Porter's flotilla landed some of its own heavy cannon and their crews to man the Benton Battery. The field gunners adapted themselves to the siege role by pushing their guns forward to achieve greater accuracy and impact.

While Pemberton kept within his own perimeter, Grant sent Blair's 2nd Division north-eastwards in response to reports of Confederate movements between the Yazoo and the Big Black. To fill the gap they left at Haynes' Bluff, he borrowed the Mississippi Marine Brigade from Porter and later described it as 'a nondescript floating force which had been assigned to his command and proved very useful'. Blair went forty-five miles up the Yazoo and was away for a week. He encountered no enemy, but destroyed bridges and roads so as to make difficulties for any relieving force. On his return, he was ordered to watch all the crossings on the Big Black and to block the roads from the east with felled trees.

Banks, who had returned from his Red River campaign and begun a siege of Port Hudson, wrote to Grant at this time, asking to be sent reinforcements. Grant declined, not wishing to weaken his own force, which might be attacked on two fronts if Pemberton attempted a sortie while Johnston was approaching with a strong relieving force. Banks, on the other hand, faced no threat of a sortie nor did it seem likely that Johnston intended going to the relief of Port Hudson. When Richmond urged him to do so, he replied that he had neither the supplies nor transport required, and that Grant could easily intercept him with a superior force while the remainder held the lines around Vicksburg.

Nathaniel Prentiss Banks (1816–1894) was essentially a 'political' general who proved unenterprising and ineffective in command.

THE CINCINNATI: MAY 1863

Sherman, with his right on the Mississippi, asked for naval gunfire support to enfilade the landward Confederate defences. Co-ordinating this with an attack by four gunboats on the batteries below the city, Porter ordered the veteran iron-clad *Cincinnati* into action on 27 May. Unconvinced by army intelligence reports that the heavy guns had been removed from the river batteries for service against the siege works, he ordered the boat to strengthen her armour by packing heavy logs and bales of hay into every available space. At 8.30 a.m., with a full head of steam, she headed downstream while her medical officer, Assistant Surgeon Richard A. Hall, was finishing a letter to his wife in Fairfield, Indiana. After telling her that because of the heat he had taken to sleeping on deck, he confided that *Cincinnati* was on her way to destroy 'a masked battery that holds General Sherman in check and … has destroyed a great number of his brave boys … He says that if the *Cincinnati* will take the battery … he and his men will go into Vicksburg. Well, we will do it for him and give him a chance.'

Cincinnati engaged a two-gun water battery with her bow guns as she approached, then her broadside as she turned and her stern guns as she turned again. It soon became clear that Vicksburg's heavy guns were still on the river. Shooting with great accuracy, they soon inflicted severe damage and dismount-ed several of *Cincinnati*'s guns. Plunging fire from the bluffs proved particularly effective, penetrating iron, hay and wood with equal ease. Two rounds reached the shell-room, one passing through the fantail, below the water-line, and rico-cheting up through the recess of the stern paddle-wheel. Another came through her side, flooding the magazine, and thus ending the supply of ammunition to

Porter's fleet on the night of 16/17 April and six nights later came under fire from Confederate artillery overlooking the Mississippi. One of these guns was this 18-pounder gun nick-named 'Whistling Dick', which also sank the Union gun-boat *Cincinnati*.

her guns. As the boat started to fill, the pilot-house in which Dr Hall had taken to spending his uncomfortable nights was hit and the starboard tiller carried away. Realising that *Cincinnati* was sinking, her captain, Lieutenant Commander George M. Bache, ran her upstream for about a mile and a half before coming alongside on the starboard bank. The wounded were taken ashore over a gang-plank and a hawser was run out to secure the boat to a tree, but enemy fire drove the mooring-party to take cover before it had been made fast. As the boat drifted out, her crew were ordered to swim ashore. Still under fire, *Cincinnati* sank in three fathoms, as Bache reported, 'with her colors nailed to the mast, or rather the stump of one, all three having been shot away'. About twenty-five of her crew were killed or wounded by shell-fire and another fifteen were drowned, with one missing.

Sherman sent a company of the 76th Ohio Infantry to help the survivors and later wrote to Porter that 'the style in which the *Cincinnati* engaged the batteries elicited universal praise'. Six Medals of Honor were eventually awarded to *Cincinnati*'s survivors, among them (in 1916!) Quartermaster Frank Bois, who had nailed the colours to the stump of her foremast. The hundreds of Vicksburg citizens who had watched the combat from their hill-tops took, quite literally, a different view. As she went down, the men cheered and the ladies waved their handkerchiefs. Mrs Balfour recorded that 'we went to see another gunboat fight, five boats from below and one a terrible monster from above engaged our batteries. In a very short time we perceived that the monster was disabled … She drifted over to the Mississippi shore … and there she lies under water except her chimneys and her horn!.' The *Daily Citizen*, Vicksburg's sole remaining newspaper, reported that 'this giant, the boasted monster and terror of the western waters, is now a total wreck in view of both friend and foe,' and complimented the shore batteries on their shooting. Among the flotsam that drifted downstream from *Cincinnati* was her surgeon's medical chest with the unsent letter to his wife. The doctor himself survived, to set up practice after the war as a gynaecologist in Wichita, Kansas, where he became a leading member of the community and eventually died of old age.

THE CONTINUED RESISTANCE

While enemy works grew steadily closer, Pemberton still hoped for help from Johnston. In messages sent before the repulse of Grant's second assault, he had said: 'An army will be necessary to save Vicksburg and that quickly. Will it not be sent? … The men credit, and are encouraged by, a report that you are near with a strong force.' On 29 May Johnston replied: 'I am too weak to save Vicksburg. Can do no more than attempt to save you and your garrison. It will be impossible to extricate you unless you co-operate and we make mutually-supporting movements.' This was followed by a series of messages between the two generals, some taking several days and crossing each other in delivery, with

Pemberton asking when and by what route Johnston would come, and Johnston stressing the need to co-ordinate their attacks and asking which route Pemberton was expecting him to use.

In a move to aid Vicksburg from the west, Major General E. Kirby Smith, commanding the Confederate Trans-Mississippi Department, concentrated two divisions under Major General Richard Taylor around Richmond, Louisiana. Early on 6 June Taylor attacked Milliken's Bend, held by the veteran 23rd Iowa Infantry with the 9th, 11th and 13 Louisiana Colored Infantry and 1st Mississippi Colored Infantry, recently raised from African-Americans. Taylor's Texan infantry advanced under heavy musketry fire and then delivered a charge that drove the defenders down to the river-side. There the Confederates came within range of the gunboats *Choctaw* and *Lexington* and were forced to take cover. A simultaneous threat to the installations at nearby Young's Point was equally unsuccessful and Taylor subsequently withdrew. He later wrote that 'with the loss of some scores of prisoners, the negroes were driven over the levees to the protection of the gunboats,' but added that nothing could have been achieved by this expedition, and that it diverted troops who might have helped save the garrison of Port Hudson.

Brigadier General Elias S. Dennis, commanding the newly formed District of North-eastern Louisiana, spoke highly of the gallantry of the African-Americans, who, despite their limited training, had stood up to the Texans in hand-to-hand fighting. African-Americans throughout the Union took a justifiable pride in this action, the first in which coloured troops fought in significant numbers. Abolitionists who had urged the employment of African-Americans as soldiers in combatant as much as in logistic roles were strengthened in their arguments. Grant himself was one of those who, previously ambivalent on the question, decided that it had proved that such men, who had not previously been given the chance to bear arms, could, under good officers, make good soldiers. After this attack on his base was beaten off, Grant strengthened Dennis' command with a brigade from Sherman's XV Corps, to keep the Confederates at a distance.

Within Vicksburg, the civilian population as well as the soldiers, were suffering the effects of continual bombardment and the growing shortage of supplies. Before marching out to meet Grant, Pemberton had ordered all civilians to leave the city, but many, confident of his success, or with nowhere else to go, remained in their homes. After his defeat, he was followed back into Vicksburg by refugees fleeing from Yankee occupation and bringing the total of civilians within the defences to some 3,000. Bombs from the mortar-boats, however, knew no distinctions of age or sex, nor between fighting men and non-combatants. Foreshadowing what would befall British and German cities in the bomber offensives of the Second World War, parents lost lives and limbs as they tried to protect their children, and infants were killed or maimed in their parents' arms. Horses and cattle died when shells landed in their scanty pastures, and domestic pets perished beside their owners or ran off in terror. Scarcely a building remained undamaged.

Most people took shelter with their families and servants in 'rat-holes', caves dug into the city's hillsides by gangs of African-Americans, who hired themselves out for this work and became experts in their construction. Some rat-holes were in the gardens of private residences, while others were organised on a communal basis, with multiple entrances and areas for laundry, cooking, or recreation. Some of the shelters were furnished in relative comfort and had adequate ventilation. Others were noisome, damp and liable to invasion by snakes and vermin of various kinds. In quiet intervals, their occupants emerged to go to their homes and note the steady destruction of their city. Some, men and women alike, were killed as they went about their daily tasks. Most families had supplies of basic foodstuffs but these began to run out as the siege continued and children especially were affected by the shortage of fresh provisions. Some of the more public-spirited among the wealthy shared what they had with poorer citizens. Others, in the commercial sector, used the opportunity for profiteering in commodities of all kinds.

Women did their best to keep themselves and their families neat, despite the manifest unsuitability of mid-Nineteenth Century fashion, with its tight bodices and full skirts and petticoats, for life under bombardment. The only compensation was that long sleeves and long skirts protected the large veins in wrists and ankles from mosquitoes and other blood-sucking insects. Cotton dresses were the normal summer wear, though there were few opportunities for changes of clothing. Some of the younger ladies sent their military acquaintances to the trenches with nosegays and held parties for them on their return. A few even rode out to the lines at dusk, when they could more easily see the burning fuses of the incoming missiles. Others were of a more nervous disposition and Captain Loughborough, an artillery officer, told his wife after a particularly heavy bombardment that one lady and her daughters had sought refuge in his adjutant's office.

The captain's wife, the 26-year-old Mary Webster Loughborough, later published her own experiences as *My Cave Life in Vicksburg*. A soldier, known to the family as Henry, was stationed near her house and became a favourite of her 2-year-old daughter. Late in the siege, he brought the child a jay to amuse her, but Mrs Loughborough's servant Cynthia, seeing the little girl had no energy, said 'Miss Mary, she's hungry; let me make her some soup from the bird.' Mary Loughborough agonised about the fate of the bird but then, thinking of her child, half-consented. Before she could change her mind, Cynthia disappeared and returned with a nourishing small meal. Not long afterwards, the same soldier, with a comrade, was trying to dismantle an unexploded shell when it blew up. Mrs Loughborough carried her terrified daughter away from the sight and later wrote 'My first impulse was to run down to them with the few remedies I possessed. Then I thought of the crowd of soldiers around the men; and if M. should come and see me there – the only lady – he might think I did wrong; so I sent my servant [perhaps the capable Cynthia] with camphor and other slight remedies I possessed, and turned into my cave with a sickened heart.' Henry, mortally wounded, was taken to hospital where he died during the night.

Cynthia was only one of the African-Americans who shared all the privations of a siege that was being undertaken in a cause that would make them free. They too were being killed or terribly wounded in the bombardment, and Mary Loughborough noted the sound of lamentation from their wives and children. Many Southerners commented on their endurance and courage under fire, qualities which, like those of the Colored Infantry at Milliken's Bend, they had not expected African-Americans to possess.

Hospitals, seemingly always the victims of bombing, were repeatedly hit, bringing death or severe injuries to surgeons and patients alike. Some inside the city thought that the enemy was deliberately firing upon the yellow quarantine flags that, in the days before the founding of the Red Cross, fluttered to mark the location of a hospital. The usual diseases associated with bad sanitation increased the sick lists, and the effects of continuous exposure in the trenches combined with poor rations to weaken resistance. Occasional storms combined with the summer heat to produce clouds of mosquitoes and with them, outbreaks of malaria. Round-the-clock bombardment from the river gave no one, sick or well, the chance of much-needed rest and relaxation. Outside the overcrowded wards, men lay in tents or private houses. Nursing was provided by some of the Vicksburg ladies and by the Catholic Sisters of Mercy, who true to their vocation, had closed their hill-side seminary and remained in the city to comfort the wounded and tend the dying.

'Coonskin' tower, a lookout station for Union sharpshooters, was constructed by Lieutenant Henry C. Foster of the 23rd Indiana Infantry, whose raccoon-fur cap earned him the nickname 'Coonskin'.

THE CONTINUED APPROACH

Outside the walls, the siege works pressed gradually closer. Each night working-parties emerged from their trenches, crept forward, dug themselves in and extended the excavations to link up with those on each side of them to form lines parallel with the defences. From the parallels, new saps (trenches that headed towards the enemy works) were dug. Working-parties were mostly drawn from special pioneer units or civilian labour groups of African-Americans who came in from the abandoned neighbouring plantations to find paid employment. Combat units also took their turn, but even the mid-western farm boys flagged as temperatures soared to 100° F in the shade. Nevertheless, as campaign veterans, they proved capable sappers in other ways, tunnelling, digging, constructing various types of shelters and trench roads, and making fascines, gabions and sap-rollers, the great wicker-work cylinders filled with earth to protect those working at the sap-heads.

Grant's staff included only four professional military engineers, the intellectual élite of any 19th-century army. These were soon reduced to three by the sickness of their chief, a number quite inadequate for siege operations along a line stretching more than fifteen miles from Haynes' Bluff to Warrenton. On the eastern side, the line of contravallation was even longer, running twenty miles from the Yazoo to the railway bridge on the Big Black. While the Volunteer engineer officers, generally civil engineers by profession, could build roads, bridges and field defences, they were not trained in the complex mathematical and scientific ways of siege-craft. Grant remembered that the USMA, West Point, like most other military academies of the time, included military engineering in the syllabus. He ordered all officers who had been trained there as cadets to assist the regular engineers. His chief commissary, Colonel Robert Macfeely, though a West Pointer, begged off, on the grounds that he had forgotten all his engineering and (in allusion to his short stature and ample girth) that the only employment he could usefully undertake in this area would be as a sap-roller. 'As soldiers require rations when working in the ditches as well as when marching and fighting,' Grant wrote, 'and as we should be sure to lose him if he was used as a sap-roller, I let him off.' Macfeely survived the war and, fatter than ever, eventually became US Commissary General.

Under their additional engineers, the Union approaches pushed steadily forward. Lacking siege mortars, Grant's men constructed coehorns (light mortars that could be moved easily from place to place) by boring out hardwood trunks and strengthening the boles with metal hoops. In the trenches, a strange camaraderie grew up between the opposing soldiers. On quiet evenings, opening their negotiations by shouts of 'Hi, Yank' or 'Hi, Reb', men would exchange newspapers and trade Union coffee for Confederate tobacco. Picquets agreed short truces between themselves, sometimes with the approval of their own officers, and warned those on the other side if they were making accidental rather than deliberate moves into danger. Outside these truces, a relentless sniping by marksmen in both armies, many of them having learnt their skill as squirrel-hunters, took the lives of any who forgot to remain under cover. Whereas Grant's men had ample supplies of artillery and small-arms ammunition, Pemberton allowed only his sharpshooters to reply to them. Confederate infantrymen complained that this left them unable to slow the advancing saps. Confederate gunners, when they opened fire from their exposed barbettes, were liable to be silenced by an immediate heavy response from the besiegers.

The Union troops, enduring no less than their Confederate enemies all the miseries of trench warfare in the intense, insect-ridden heat, suffered their own share of death, wounds and sickness. Nevertheless, the worst scandals of their inadequate hospitals during the previous winter had been ameliorated by the efforts of voluntary Christian or Sanitary Commissions. Doctors complained about having to live and work in tents that were alternately too wet or too hot, but it was generally thought that their patients were better off there than being crowded inside insanitary buildings. Some ladies from the Commissions stayed to share in the nursing, though perforce not as many as those inside Vicksburg, whom the besiegers could see going to and from the hospitals in the intervals between the bombardments. Not for the first or last time in this war, Union soldiers admired the courage of their Confederate foes, women as well as men, and said it was worthy of a better cause.

Within the defences, provisions grew ever more scanty. The pie shops and other eating-places where soldiers had gone to supplement what they were given by the regimental cooks had long closed down. On 4 June Pemberton ordered that all stores of food in the city be pooled and rations be issued to the garrison and civilians alike. There was little corn left and it was replaced by local 'peas', pulses normally used as cattle-feed, but which could be made into bread of a sort if ground up and baked for several hours. Early in the siege, Union prisoners of war had been paroled and sent across the river to avoid the need to feed them. At the same time hundreds of mules for whom there was no forage had been driven outside the lines, an act of humanity, as conventionally they would have been killed or hamstrung to prevent them being of use to the enemy. Now, many of those left were slaughtered for meat. A Union naval officer commented that eating mules might impart even greater stubbornness to the defenders. Rats, the traditional fare of starving cities, were said to have appeared on various menus. Even a camel, which had lived happily at Vicksburg after the failure of President Polk's scheme to introduce these animals into the dry South-West, was turned into steaks, after being shot by a Union sniper. On half-rations, the soldiers' daily issue was four ounces of either poor quality bacon or flour and another ten of peas, rice or sugar. Although the occupants of some houses had enough supplies of ground-water for an evening cold bath, others relied on ditches and streams. Fresh water from hill-side springs was also rationed. One local woman sold the water from the well on her farm. When her husband returned from duty with his regiment in the trenches, a comrade noted that 'he walloped her good for meanness', though she may simply have been trying to eke out the income of a family dependant on a soldier's wage, paid in depreciating Confederate dollars.

In the besiegers' camp there was a sensation following a congratulatory Order to his own Corps by McClernand. Calling his men 'The Army of the Mississippi', he praised them for their bravery and past success, an unexceptional proceeding had he not also made it obvious that he attributed this to his own ability as a general. He went on to say that their attack on 22 May would have taken Vicksburg if they had been supported by the rest of the army. He copied it to the newspapers and, when copies of the Memphis *Evening Bulletin* for 13 June reached the camp, the rest of the army raised violent objections. Sherman complained to Grant that McClernand's so-called Order was 'manifestly addressed, not to an Army, but to a constituency in Illinois' and added that it 'perverts the Truth, to the ends of flattery and Self-glorification'. McPherson wrote that McClernand's account of the 22 May was 'manifestly at variance with the facts' and that 'though "born a Warrior" as he himself has stated, he has evidently forgotten one of the most essential qualities, viz. justice to others'. When called upon for an explanation, McClernand stood by his remarks, but could not justify his breach of War Department (and Grant's own) regulations against giving statements to the Press.

The two generals had been on increasingly bad terms throughout the campaign, Grant having no faith in McClernand's military ability and McClernand resentful at being deprived of the separate command he had been promised. Grant had been reluctant to remove such a well-connected and senior officer, but now he had clear evidence against him. On 18 June he relieved McClernand from command and ordered him to proceed to anywhere of his choice in the State of Illinois before reporting by letter to Army Headquarters in Washington. Command of XIII Corps was given to Major General Edward Ord, a West Pointer whom Grant liked and trusted and who had joined the army at Vicksburg two days earlier.

McClernand complied but appealed to Lincoln, who urged him to accept Grant's decision for the sake of the public good. His departure was widely welcomed by other officers, not least because, if Grant had become a casualty, command of the Army of the Tennessee would have devolved upon McClernand as the next senior ranking officer. Such an eventuality was by no means a remote one, as Grant had a habit of going into the forward positions and (to the irritation of the occupants) drawing sniper fire by incautiously looking over the parapets. Even a fall from a startled horse, such as could happen to any mounted officer, and indeed did to Grant shortly after the Vicksburg campaign, might have removed him from duty.

Grant knew that Johnston had gathered a significant force between Jackson and Canton and anticipated that he would be under pressure from Richmond to march to Vicksburg's relief. He therefore tested the city's defences ever harder. While declaring publicly that, if a relieving army came, it would be let into the city merely to swell the numbers that would eventually have to surrender, Grant countered its approach by forming an Army of Observation, under Sherman's command. On 20 June all 220 of Grant's siege and field guns, supported by gunboats and mortar-boats from the river, opened the heaviest fire of the siege, now into its thirty-fourth day. The bombardment was expected, as Confederate observers had broken the code used by Porter in signalling to his units. Mary Loughborough's husband insisted on her moving into their cave with their daughter and servants. Scarcely had she done so when a mortar-bomb rolled into the entrance. Their servant George rushed out and extinguished its fuse before it could detonate. His mistress insisted in leaving the now harmless projectile in place as evidence of his bravery. While the bombs and shells rained down, Porter released hydrogen balloons to drift over the city with 'psy-ops' leaflets, telling the enlisted men that only their officers would be remembered after the siege; that they were being duped into fighting for the Southern aristocracy, not the Southern people, and that various relieving armies, including that of Johnston himself, had been put to flight. In response, the *Daily Citizen* thanked 'Dr Porter' for entertaining the city with his fireworks displays.

THE THIRD ASSAULT: 25 JUNE 1863

Two days later, Grant's sappers reached the outer wall of the 3rd Louisiana Redoubt. The engineer responsible for this sector, Captain Andrew Hickenlooper, formed a mining section of thirty-five former colliers and began tunnelling. Working in continuous shifts and listening for Confederate countermines, they completed their task on 25 June and, following another intense bombardment, sprung their mine, containing 2,200 pounds of gunpowder, at 3.30 p.m. With Hickenlooper carrying out the conventional engineer officer's duty of leading them to the assault, the 45th Illinois Infantry rushed into the breached redoubt. Although the explosion had been an impressive sight, with earth, timber and gun-carriages thrown high into the air, the redoubt had been lightly manned and only six defenders perished. The back of the redoubt had been closed by another defence wall from which the Louisiana infantry poured a relentless fire into the assaulting troops.

Hickenlooper and his pioneers cleared a way through the debris and brought up logs for protection, but Confederate musketry and grenades turned the wood into splinters and continued to inflict casualties. At 6 p.m. the 45th were relieved in the crater by the 20th Illinois Infantry, and then, successively during the night, by the 31st and 56th Illinois and the 23rd Indiana. At daylight, the 45th returned and fought on until 10 a.m., when their place was taken by the 124th Illinois. At 5 p.m., after Hickenlooper's attempts to build a forward gun position from which to breach the wall behind the redoubt had failed, Grant ordered a withdrawal. The defenders had suffered 94 casualties. The attackers had lost some 34 killed and 209 wounded. Vicksburg had still not been taken.

THE FINAL WEEKS

Nevertheless, the situation within the city now seemed hopeless. Most of the picks and spades used for the construction and repair of defences were worn out or broken. Regiments hoarded their own despite orders to place them in a common pool for use where most needed. Morale, high when the troops were actually in combat, sagged behind the lines. The *Daily Citizen*, reduced to printing its editions on wallpaper, reported cases of undisciplined soldiers breaking into civilian premises and openly stealing animals, fruit, and other provisions. One respectable resident, William Porter, killed a thieving soldier and wounded one or two others, to the *Daily Citizen*'s evident approval. Shelling, bombing and sniping took a steady toll of casualties, including on 27 June Brigadier General Martin E. Green, the senior Confederate officer to fall during the siege. Some 6,000 men (20 per cent of Pemberton's bayonet strength) were in hospital or, fearing the contagious illnesses rife within them, had found shelter staying with their families or friends. One of the most feared diseases was erysipelas, an infection of the skin, whose common name 'St Anthony's Fire' accurately described the painful intensity of the rash that it produced. Scurvy had begun to appear among the troops,

One of the Confederate batteries defending Vicksburg, within the city's formidable natural defences.

and there was an outbreak of measles, for which neat corn whiskey was the only prescribed medicine. The City Guard, Vicksburg's citizen volunteer force, commandeered whiskey from the liquor shops for use in the hospitals, but its members were suspected of drinking much of it themselves. By the end of June five of *Cincinnati*'s guns had been recovered, despite furious cannonading by the Confederate artillery, and were brought into action as siege batteries. All along the front, the sap-heads approached to within yards of the defenders' works.

While the despairing city looked in vain for Johnston, that officer remained firm in his original appreciation that the most he could do was to save the garrison, not the place. On 12 June he told the Confederate government: 'I consider saving Vicksburg hopeless,' and said that it had to choose between losing Mississippi or Tennessee. The reply from Richmond was that 'Vicksburg must not be lost without a desperate struggle. The interest and honor of the Confederacy forbid it.' Johnston's response was to point out that Grant's position, protected by the line of contravallation and by the Big Black, was virtually impregnable. His own army alone was too small to defeat Grant and communication difficulties meant that he could not co-ordinate any attack with a sortie by Pemberton. On the other hand, he said, if he was defeated in attempting to relieve Vicksburg as ordered, both Mississippi and Alabama would be left open to a Union advance.

At the same time, Johnston pursued a quarrel with Richmond over the extent of his own authority. The view there was that if he needed more troops, he had the power as commander of the entire Western Department to take them from Bragg's Army of Tennessee. Johnston maintained that, on being assigned to the field command in Mississippi, he was no longer commanding in Tennessee. Jefferson Davis personally told him that he was still responsible for the whole Department but Johnston argued that no general could exercise the operational command of two widely separate armies. It was for this reason, he said, that he regarded himself as having been given a new assignment. His nice sense of military etiquette and his readiness to be aggrieved were illustrated by his supporting argument: 'The orders of the War Department transferring three separate bodies of troops from General Bragg's army to this, two of them without my knowledge and all of them without consulting me, would have convinced me, had I doubted.'

On 22 June Johnston wrote to Pemberton: 'General Taylor is sent by General E. K. Smith to co-operate with you from the west bank of the river, to throw in supplies to Vicksburg, and to cross with his forces if expedient and practicable.' For himself, he promised that in a few days he would try to make a demonstration in support, but had insufficient forces to do more. In the worst case, he said, rather than surrender, Pemberton was to try to cross the river at the last moment and link up with Taylor. Pemberton began to build a large number of skiffs, but Taylor, defeated at Milliken's Bend, never returned. Had he done so, he would have found the roads difficult and the country denuded of supplies all the way from Lake Providence to Bruinsburg. Even if Pemberton had tried to cross, his cockleshells would have been blown out of the water by Porter's gunboats. When coal ran short, the ever-resourceful admiral prepared to sink the skiffs by swamping them with the paddle-wheels of his transports. Along the bank, he placed sixty tar barrels and other lights in case of an attempted night crossing.

The only threat from Kirby Smith's Department lay far to the north, where Major General Sterling Price was moving from Little Rock, Arkansas, with one cavalry and one infantry division to attack Grant's supply base at Helena. Slowed by heavy rains, Price did not reach the area until 3 July, giving the Union garrison (one cavalry and two infantry brigades from what had become Ord's Corps) ample time to prepare strong defences supported by the gunboat *Tyler*. The attack was made the next day, but was repulsed after heavy fighting. By then, Vicksburg was beyond help.

Major General Sterling Price (1809–1867) served a term as Governor of the State of Missouri from 1853 to 1857.

Johnston at last succeeded in gathering the wagons and teams he needed to move on Vicksburg. He expected the garrison to come out to join him, but appreciated that it would have only the food or ammunition that remained in its packs and pouches after fighting its way through Grant's lines. He therefore needed to carry supplies for the troops from Vicksburg as well as for his own men. After spending the first few days of July in a detailed reconnaissance, he sent a message to Pemberton to say that he would make the promised diversion on 7 July. His plan was to pass through Edwards and advance along an axis south of the railway, where Grant's lines seemed less strong. With him would go 32,000 men, made up of 20,000 infantry; 2,000 cavalry; field artillery; the supply wagons and a bridging train with which to cross the Big Black. On 2 July, in response to reports that Johnston was on the move, a brigade of Union infantry made a forced march through intense heat to counter his advance.

THE CAPITULATION

For Vicksburg, however, time had run out. Dora Richards Miller, the young wife of an attorney and, like him, a secret sympathiser with the Union cause, had endured most of the siege courageously. By 30 June, eight months pregnant with her first child and fearing that, like so many others, she would be killed or lose a limb to the flying shell fragments, she could take no more. Lawyer-like, her husband, knowing that as an able-bodied man he would have to remain himself, decided to try making use of the Danish passport (Dora had been born on the Danish West Indian island of St Croix) that she had prudently obtained for just such a contingency. An officer went out with a flag of truce to plead for her departure, but returned, flushed and angry, with the message 'General Grant says that no human being shall pass out of Vicksburg; but the lady may feel sure danger will soon be over. Vicksburg will surrender on the Fourth.' The Fourth of July, American Independence Day, assumed a growing significance. Some Union troops in the trenches, expecting the siege to continue for weeks to come, were surprised to learn from enemy picquets that Grant had made this his target date for taking the city. Others had already agreed among themselves that this would indeed be the ideal date. There was also talk of the Confederates planning to take advantage of this by making a sortie on the same day. The *Daily Citizen*, defiant to the last, reported on 2 July: 'The great Ulysses – the Yankee Generalissimo, surnamed Grant – has expressed his intention of dining in Vicksburg on Saturday next ... Ulysses must get into the city before he dines in it. The way to cook a rabbit is ... first catch the rabbit.'

Pemberton had already considered the inevitability of a capitulation. In his dispatch to Johnston of 22 June he had suggested that, if no relief was possible, Johnston should approach Grant for terms that would allow the surrender of the city, but not the garrison. Johnston was not prepared to do this, as Grant would immediately recognise it as evidence of Johnston's weakness. Instead, he passed the responsibility back to Pemberton and gave him authority to negotiate a surrender if the time came. On the evening of 2 July Pemberton wrote to his four divisional commanders to say that, with no prospects of the siege being raised and few of supplies being thrown in, it would soon become necessary to evacuate Vicksburg. He asked them to report on the condition of their troops and their ability to undertake a successful evacuation.

When they assembled the next day, the general opinion was that the men had the spirit to continue fighting behind their defences, but lacked the physical strength for a long march or an encounter with the enemy in the field. Six thousand men were on the sick list. Of those in the trenches, only 11,000 were fit for duty. Many men had deserted and asked Grant to send them north where they could find work to support themselves and their families. There were two million rounds of small-arms ammunition left, but food was almost gone. Some of the soldiers had come to depend on scraps from civilian households to eke out what the commissaries issued. Forage was so short that the horses in the artillery teams could scarcely pull the guns. Medical supplies were almost exhausted. With his own troops unable to reach Johnston, who was adamant that he himself could not reach the city, there was no point in holding out any longer. The only real question was when to surrender. At their conference, Pemberton told his assembled generals, 'I am a Northern man. I know my people. I know we can get better terms from them on the Fourth of July than any other day of the year.'

On Friday 3 July, after forty-seven days of siege, he sent Bowen with a flag of truce to ask for an armistice in order to prevent needless further bloodshed and to discuss the terms of a surrender. Bowen had been a neighbour of Grant's in Missouri before the war and asked to see him, but, in accordance with military etiquette, was met by an officer of equal status as a divisional commander, Brigadier General Andrew J. Smith. Grant agreed to meet Pemberton later in the day and sent Bowen back with a written reply, saying that Pemberton could end any further bloodshed whenever he chose, 'by the unconditional surrender of the city and garrison', but adding 'Men who have shown so much endurance and courage as those now in Vicksburg, will always challenge the respect of an adversary, and I can assure you will be treated with all the respect due to prisoners of war.'

At their subsequent meeting, Grant greeted Pemberton politely as an old comrade of the Mexican War, but declined to offer any alteration in the terms offered. Pemberton, 'rather snappishly' in Grant's recollection, replied that the conference might as well end and turned as though to leave. Bowen, however, to keep the negotiations going, suggested that he continue discussions with Smith. Grant agreed, on condition that he would not be bound by them, and the two army commanders sat down under an oak tree, exchanging no more than civilities, Grant with his unlit cigar, Pemberton chewing a blade of grass. Bowen, who was to die of fever a few days later, asked for the garrison to be allowed to march out with its guns and small arms. When this was rejected, the conversations ended and the Confederates returned to their own lines. Grant promised that he would offer his final terms later that night and would send word to Porter to stop his bombardment while the negotiations continued.

Grant then called what he described as the nearest approach to a council of war that he had ever held, to invite comments on the terms he intended to offer. He told his generals that he would retain the final decision in his own hands and, when almost all of them indicated that they did not support the proposed terms, ignored their opinion accordingly. The garrison would be allowed to surrender with the promise that all those who undertook not to serve again until properly exchanged would be released on parole. Weapons and public property were to be left behind, but all officers would be allowed to retain their side-arms and personal baggage, and mounted officers allowed one horse each. The rank and file would be allowed all their clothing, but no other property. Thirty wagons each with four horses or mules would be allowed for the transport of such items as could not be carried by the men. The garrison could take whatever food it had left and the necessary cooking equipment. Pemberton had told Grant that there were two weeks' supplies left, but in fact the Union commissaries were soon issuing rations to the surrendered garrison. All slaves held within the Confederate lines were declared free as soon as Vicksburg surrendered, but those belonging to the officers were allowed to remain with their former masters if they so wished, as many had grown up as members of their families.

The only concession that Pemberton secured was that, before the Union troops marched in, the garrison would march out, stack its weapons and colours and then return to their camps, so that it could not be said that an enemy had entered while they actually held the walls. Grant reckoned that men spared needless humiliation would prove less bitter enemies while the war lasted and better citizens when it was over, and the terms of the surrender at Vicksburg foreshadowed those he would give to Robert E. Lee at Appomattox Court House nearly two years later. Moreover, by releasing them on parole, he avoided the strain that guarding, feeding and transporting thirty thousand men would have placed on his own resources. He would not, however, accept Pemberton's stipulations regarding the rights and property of the citizens, not because he wished to do them harm (in fact, he gave strict orders that they should not be molested, and hanged some of his own men who murdered a householder) but because he could not accept a formal limitation on what might be required by military necessity. Pemberton then held his final council of war. Some members were for cutting their way out or holding their lines until they had eaten the last mule or dog, but the majority accepted the inevitable. At dawn white flags were displayed all along the front to signify that Grant's terms had been accepted.

THE ENTRY INTO VICKSBURG: 4 JULY 1863

At 10 a.m. on Saturday 4 July 1863 the garrison of Vicksburg, after being reviewed by its commander, marched out with colours flying and bands playing, stacked its arms and marched back to its camps in good order. For the most part, their opponents watched them with silent respect, though Major Lockett, whose works had withstood every attack, heard the men of one Union division give a hearty cheer 'for the gallant defenders'. Logan's Division, which had borne so much of the burden of the siege and the preceding battles, was the first to enter the city with its own bands playing and regimental colours flying, one of which, that of the 45th Illinois Infantry, was soon hoisted over the court-house. A regimental chaplain, remembering how his men made every effort to appear at their smartest for the occasion, noted that the city still seemed far distant as they marched the three miles in from their camp, through the heat of a July noon. He

John Logan (1826–1886) was a congressman when the war broke out and served at First Bull Run. He became a senator in 1871 and stood unsuccessfully for the vice presidency in 1884.

noted too that not a dog barked nor a cat slunk away at their passing and supposed that all had been eaten. Grant and his staff rode in to receive Pemberton's formal surrender but were received with few of the conventional courtesies. Pemberton offered his sword and was invited to retain it. Grant asked for a glass of water and was merely told where one might be found. Lockett and some other officers provided better examples of Southern politeness and gratefully accepted Yankee cigars, whiskey and provisions. Ordinary Union soldiers too were willing to fraternise with those whom only starvation had defeated. 'I myself', Grant later recalled, 'saw our men taking bread from their haversacks and giving it to the enemy they had so recently been engaged in starving out.'

Having accepted the surrender, Grant, always careful to observe the etiquette of naval-military relations, rode down to the riverside, once again to exchange congratulations with Rear-Admiral Porter. Together, they watched the flotilla pass the now silent batteries that had defied it for so long. A long procession of war vessels and transports steamed past, with flags and streamers fluttering, calliopes playing and whistles at full blast. The review over, some of the transports tied up along the river front and began unloading stores for the starving city. In the *Daily Citizen*'s abandoned offices, Union troops found the copy for Thursday 2 July 1863 still set up in type. They added an extra paragraph and issued the last of the wallpaper editions, with the suggestion that it might one day be valued as a curiosity: 'Two days bring about great changes. The banner of the Union floats above Vicksburg. General Grant has "caught the rabbit"; he has dined in Vicksburg and he did bring his dinner with him.'

With Vicksburg, Grant captured 31,000 Confederate soldiers, 172 pieces of artillery and 60,000 stands of small arms. During the actual siege, he lost 766 men killed and 4,063 wounded and missing, against Pemberton's 875 killed and 2,327 wounded and missing. Grant wrote to Banks, besieging Port Hudson, notifying him of Vicksburg's fall and saying that he would send him all the troops he needed to take what had become the only remaining Confederate foothold on the east bank of the Mississippi. Banks printed an edited version and distributed it as a morale-booster for his own men. A copy reached Major General Gardner, commanding the Confederate garrison of Port Hudson, who sent to Banks to say that if Vicksburg had indeed surrendered, it would be useless for Port Hudson to hold out any longer. On being assured by Banks that the report was correct, Gardner surrendered unconditionally on 9 July with 6,000 men, 51 guns, 5,000 small arms and all his stores. Lincoln, with his gift for words, declared 'The Father of Waters once more goes unvexed to the sea.'

With the fall of Vicksburg, the Mississippi became a Union waterway, and the victors could turn their full attention to settling affairs farther east.

7
CONCLUSION

The Vicksburg campaign has been fairly described as the Civil War in microcosm. On the Confederate side, the aim was to hold out against superior numbers and technology until the enemy grew tired, or until help came from an outside source. On the Union side, the problem was one of overcoming the difficulties of distance, terrain and climate to bring that superiority to bear in the face of a determined resistance.

In the war as a whole, just as at Vicksburg, the decisive victory was won by Ulysses Simpson Grant, who was summoned by Lincoln to Washington to become General-in-Chief in March 1864. After taking personal command of the Army of the Potomac, as he had that of the Army of the Tennessee, he eventually defeated Robert E. Lee's Army of Northern Virginia by the same strategy he had used at Vicksburg, combining success in battle with starvation and economic warfare behind the lines. Sherman, who succeeded him in command of the Army of the Tennessee, followed Grant's example by disregarding supply lines and living off the enemy's country in his march to the sea in January 1864. He accepted Joseph E. Johnston's surrender of the last Confederate army in the field seventeen days after Grant accepted that of Lee at Appomattox Court House.

Although it was his victories around Richmond that decided the war, Grant's Vicksburg campaign is the one that shines with the greatest brilliance. His appreciation of the political imperative of advancing from Milliken's Bend rather than retreating to Memphis and renewing a land offensive; his deception plans of attacking through the bayous and from the Yazoo; his cavalry raids (especially Grierson's ride) to distract the enemy's attention from the critical point; his gamble in sending the gunboats past Vicksburg on a journey of no return and landing his army where, had he been defeated, there was no retreat except into the river; his decision to abandon his base and march through enemy territory to a point from where he could again be supplied; his use of rapid movement to prevent the enemy concentrating against him and his application of overwhelming force at the vital moment can all be compared with the genius of a Napoleon. Indeed, they can be better compared with that of a Wellington who, at the operational level, conducted several hard-fought sieges and, at the strategic level relied upon a Navy that his opponent could never match. On the river, as on the sea-coast, Union naval superiority denied the Confederates both the logistic benefits of water transport and the tactical ones of heavy gunfire delivered at close range.

In Grant's own words: 'The navy under Porter was all it could be, during the entire campaign. Without its assistance the campaign could not have been successfully made with twice the number of men engaged. It could not have been made at all, in the way that it was, with any number of men, without such assistance. The most perfect harmony reigned between the two arms of the service. There was never a request made, that I am aware of, either of the flag-officer or any of his subordinates, that was not promptly complied with.'

At Vicksburg, Grant was fortunate in his opponents. It cannot be denied that at times so too were Napoleon and Wellington. Nevertheless, Napoleon himself would ask of any general 'is he lucky?', and the motto in Wellington's coat of arms translates as 'Fortune favours the Brave'. Pemberton, as a professional soldier, decided that, unaided, he could not defeat Grant's superior numbers. A military engineer by training, he was prepared to rely on Vicksburg's defences until relief should come, contrary to the axiom that a general retreating into a fortress is like a drowning man clinging to an anchor. His superior, Johnston, a better general, was prepared to sacrifice any position, no matter how prestigious, for the sake of an advantage in the field. The divided Confederate counsels in the Vicksburg campaign echoed those that bedevilled the Confederacy as a whole. Pemberton was ordered by his Government to hold Vicksburg and by his superior to abandon it. Johnston received no satisfactory answer to the question of which was to be given priority, Mississippi or Tennessee. Reinforcements from the east were too little and too late. Help from the west never came at all.

The day after Vicksburg surrendered, the Army of Northern Virginia began its retreat from the bloody field of Gettysburg, Pennsylvania. Although that is the more famous battle, generally regarded as marking the turning-point of the war and listed among the world's decisive combats accordingly, it was at Vicksburg that the Union achieved the clearer victory. After Gettysburg, Lee still had an army in the field and his opponents were too exhausted to press home their advantage. At Vicksburg, Pemberton lost his entire army together with the city and Grant was able to turn immediately against the outnumbered Johnston. The psychological impact was profound. Jefferson Davis had declared that Vicksburg, the nail-head of the Confederacy, could not fall, and his prestige slumped. Lincoln, the key to the Mississippi now in his pocket, took new heart. The South was divided into its two halves. Although the gunboats, with only one for every ten miles and only fifty landing-places on the lower river, could not patrol every bend and though the Confederates could still cross in small numbers, or harass passing traffic, the water road to the sea was opened. A week after the surrender of Port Hudson, with many of Vicksburg's citizens having become refugees, and many of Pemberton's soldiers straggling towards their homes (some never to rejoin their colours) the river-boat *Imperial* reached New Orleans, having steamed the twelve hundred miles from St Louis without hindrance.

To Grant, Lincoln wrote: 'I write this now as a grateful acknowledgement for the inestimable service you have done the country.' But Grant's victory at Vicksburg did not lead directly to his appointment as general in command of all the Union armies. It would take another battle, at Chattanooga in November 1863, to persuade Lincoln that this was the man to face Robert E. Lee.

SELECT BIBLIOGRAPHY

Arnold, James R. *The Armies of U. S. Grant*. London, 1995

Ballard, Michael B. *The Campaign for Vicksburg*. Fort Washington, PA, 1996

Bearss, Edwin C. *The Vicksburg Campaign*, 3 vols. Dayton, Ohio, 1981

Boynton, Charles B. *The History of the Navy during the Rebellion*, 2 vols. New York, 1868

Brown, D. Alexander. *Grierson's Raid*. Urbana, Illinois, 1954

Carter, Samuel. *The final fortress: The Campaign for Vicksburg, 1862–1863*. New York, 1980

Dana, Charles A. *Recollections of the Civil War*. New York, 1898

Davis, George B. (ed.). *The Official History of the Civil War*. Washington, D.C., 1891–95. (re-published New York, 1958)

Donovan, Timothy H. (ed.). *The American Civil War*. USMA West Point, New York, 1986

Downs, Tom (ed.). *Louisiana and the Deep South*. Lonely Planet series, London, 2001

Eicher, David J. *The Longest Night: A Military History of the Civil War*. London, 2002

Grabau, Warren E. *98 Days. A Geographer's View of the Vicksburg Campaign*. Knoxville, Tenn., 2002

Grant, Ulysses Simpson. *Personal Memoirs*. New York, 1996 (first pub. Hartford, CT., 1885)

Hankinson, Alan. *Vicksburg 1863: Grant Clears the Mississippi*. London, 1993

Heathcote, T. A. 'Vicksburg 1863', unattributed chapter in Holmes, Richard. *Epic Land Battles*. London, 1976

Hoehling, A. A. *Vicksburg: 47 Days of Siege*. Mechanicsburg, PA., 1969

Howarth, Stephen. *To Shining Sea: A History of the United States Navy 1775–1991*. London, 1991

Johnson, R. U., and Buel, C. C. (eds.). *Battles and Leaders of the Civil War*. 4 vols. New York, 1884

Johnston, Joseph E. *Narrative of Military Operations directed during the late war between the States by Joseph E Johnston, General, CSA*. Bloomington, Indiana, 1959

Kennedy, Frances H. (ed.). *The Civil War Battlefield Guide*. Boston, Mass., 1990

McFeeley, William S. *Grant: A Biography*. New York, 1981

Martin, Christopher. *Damn the Torpedoes: The Story of America's First Admiral, David Glasgow Farragut*. New York, 1970

Miess, Earl S. *The Web of Victory: Grant at Vicksburg*. Baton Rouge, La., 1955

Mitchell, Joseph B. *Decisive Battles of the Civil War*. New York, 1962

Pemberton, John C. *Pemberton: Defender of Vicksburg*. Chapel Hill, North Carolina, 1942

Porter, David D. *Incidents and Anecdotes of the Civil War*. New York, 1886
— *Naval History of the Civil War*. New York, 1886

Register, Paul J. *Vicksburg Park Busts and Statues*. Vicksburg, 1997

Schultz, Duane. *The Most Glorious Fourth. Vicksburg and Gettysburg*. New York, 2002

Sheffield, Gary. 'Nailhead of the South. Siege of Vicksburg, 1863', in *Military Illustrated*. London, September 1994

Sherman, William Tecumseh. *Memoirs*. 2 vols. New York, 1875

Sifakis, Stewart. *Who was Who in the Civil War*. New York, 1988

Spencer, James. *Civil War Generals: Categorised Listings and Biographical Directory*. New York, 1986

Spiller, Roger J. (ed.). *Dictionary of American Military Biography*. 3 vols. Connecticut, 1984

United States National Park Service. *Vicksburg and the opening of the Mississippi River, 1862–63*. (NPS Handbook no. 137), Vicksburg, 1986

Watson, J. Wreford. *North America: Its countries and regions*, London. 1963

Welcher, Frank J. *The Union Army 1861–1865, Organisation and Operations*, vol II, *The Western Theatre*. Bloomington, Indiana, 1993

Wheeler, Richard. *The Siege of Vicksburg*. London, 1991

Winschel, Terence J. *Triumph or Defeat. The Vicksburg Campaign*. Mason City, Iowa, 1999

Confederate ammunition. The South, less industrialised than the North, used a great variety of rifled projectiles because ordnance had to be procured as and when possible. Some seventy different types of projectiles were in use at one time.

THE BATTLEFIELD TODAY

TOURS AND MUSEUMS

In general, the terrain in which the Vicksburg campaign was fought remains much as it has been for ages past, with flat, swampy ground on the western side of the Mississippi River and low, rolling hills, punctuated by steep ravines and canebrakes, on the eastern side. The major change in the appearance of the countryside is the result of cotton no longer being the profitable staple crop that it once was, so that many of the open fields through which the Civil War soldiers marched are now covered with trees and used for forestry or shooting (American 'hunting'). Nevertheless, the site of the battle of the Big Black crossing is still cultivated farmland, as are many of the stretches along the Yazoo where Sherman made his unsuccessful landings.

The most noticeable alterations in the landscape have been caused by the restless Mississippi itself, which has either washed away or retreated from several of the waterside sites, such as Young's Point, Bruinsburg and Grand Gulf, that played an important part in the story of the campaign. Nowhere has this had greater impact than at Vicksburg itself, where less than ten years after the battle the river finally broke through the De Soto Peninsula, just to the north-east of Grant's canal, and carved out the new bed that Lincoln had expected. The old bed was left as a backwater, which was subsequently joined to the Yazoo by a broad canal.

The Vicksburg National Military Park and Cemetery preserves 1,858 acres of the north-eastern quarter of the siege site, including both Confederate and Union positions. The Visitor Center at the entrance to the park has the usual facilities, bookshop, explanatory film, etc, and leads to a well-marked tourist trail

containing 26 State monuments, 20 statues, 63 busts, and dozens of smaller memorials, pieces of artillery, etc. The gunboat *Cairo* (locally pronounced Kay-roe) has been raised and placed on exhibition within the park, but is currently closed to visitors pending the outcome of litigation. The park is open daily, except at Christmas, and re-enactments of episodes in the siege take place during May and July. In many places, groves of trees were planted to stabilise the remaining earthworks and although they give a pleasing appearance, resembling the surroundings of a great country house, they tend to obscure the sight-lines of what was, during the siege, open ground. Recently, it has been discovered that the roots of the mature trees actually loosen the soft, sandy soil of the area, with the result that the Park authorities now plan gradually to replace the trees with an appropriate species of grass. This, though opposed by a number of environmentalists, should do much to restore the historic appearance of the battlefield.

The city of Vicksburg contains a number of ante-bellum buildings, including the Old Court House, open to the public as historic houses or museums.

Organised coach (American 'bus') visits to the Vicksburg battlefields are periodically available through travel companies specialising in military or historical tours. River boats still call at Vicksburg as they pass between New Orleans and Memphis, but are as much of a luxurious way of travelling as they ever were, and suit only those with ample time and funds at their disposal. Visitors travelling independently will normally go to the area by car along Highway 61, from the direction of either New Orleans or Memphis, the nearest two large airports. The Friends of the Vicksburg Campaign and Historic Trail, Inc., in association with the Mississippi Department of Archives and History, produce an authoritative and well-illustrated pamphlet containing sketch-maps and details of a recommended itinerary. This features a tour of eighteen stops, including sites at Grand Gulf, Port Gibson, Raymond, Jackson, Edwards and Vicksburg itself.

The 2nd, 4th and 6th Massachusetts Light Artillery were among the troops from New England who captured New Orleans. Here they are seen at Baton Rouge in May 1862. By the end of the campaign, their numbers had been reduced by exhaustion, malaria and scurvy from 3,200 to 800 men fit for duty.

INDEX

Arkansas, 43–6
Arkansas Post, see Fort Hindman
Army of the Tennessee, formation of, 53
assaults on Vicksburg, 99–104, 114
Baker's Creek, see Champion Hill
Big Black River, 90–95
Brown, Isaac Newton, 28, 43
Carondelet, 36, 37, 40–4, 62, 63, 71, 77, 81
casualties, 44, 45, 50, 52, 76, 80, 82, 83, 89, 92, 101, 114, 115, 121
Champion Hill, 84–9
Chickasaw Bluffs, 48–51
Cincinnati, 36, 40, 41, 44, 52, 62, 63, 106, 107, 116
Dana, Charles Anderson, 68
Davis, Jefferson, 14, 15, 16, 22, 23, 24, 51, 57, 69, 74, 75, 85, 97, 116, 123
Davis, Charles H, 26, 28, 40–5, 47
Deer Creek, 61–5
defences of Vicksburg, 96–9
De Soto peninsula and canal, 8, 12, 41, 45, 53, 61, 62, 68, 99, 126
Duckport, 68, 69
Ellet, Charles (Junior), 27, 41
Ellet, Charles R., 43, 56, 67,
evacuation of Vicksburg considereed by Confederates, 97
Farragut, David G., 25, 38–45, 57, 65–9, 94, 124
Foote, Andrew H., 26, 37
Forrest, Nathan Bedford, 72, 75, 83
Fort Hindman, 51–2
Fort Pemberton, 60–3, 67
Fort Pillow, 34, 40, 41
Grand Gulf, 81–3
Grant, Ulysses Simpson: commands Army of the Tennessee and tasked with capture of Vicksburg, 47; plan for Sherman to attack from the Yazoo, 48; abandons offensive after Van Dorn's raid, 48; and the Fort Hindman expedition, 51; takes command of unified Union army at Young's Point, 53; strategic considerations, 53–4; and De Soto canal, 53–4; and Lake Providence waterway,

54, and the Yazoo Pass, 54–5, 68; and the Fort Pemberton expedition, 61; marches army from Milliken's Bend to New Carthage, 68–9, 72; launches Grierson's raid, 73; crosses Mississippi at Bruinsburg, 79–81; takes Grand Gulf, 81–2; advances on Jackson, 83; at Battle of Champion Hill, 86–9; decides to storm Vicksburg, 99; attempts assaults on the city, 99–104; decides on a siege, 104; relieves McClernand of command, 113; launches a third assault on Vicksburg, 114; sets 4 July as his target date for taking the city, 118; and terms for surrender, 118–20; enters Vicksburg, 120; his victory assessed, 122–3
Grierson, Benjamin Henry, 73–6, 80, 83, 122
Halleck, Henry, 17–21, 47, 51, 53, 82, 103, 105
Holly Springs, 48
Hurlbut, Stephen A., 20, 29, 53, 72, 99
Indianola, 56, 57, 58, 65
Island No. 10, 34, 37
Johnston, Joseph E., 19, 21–3, 32, 38, 52, 69, 74, 75, 80, 81, 83, 84, 85, 86, 88, 89, 91, 96, 97, 100, 104, 105, 107, 108, 113–18, 122–4
Lee, Robert E., 22, 23, 26, 119, 122, 123
Lee, Samuel Phillips, 26, 39, 42
Lincoln, Abraham, 13–17, 19, 25, 46, 47, 52–4, 68, 113, 121–3, 126
Lockett, Samuel H., 96, 104, 120
McClernand, John A., 19, 21, 29, 47–53, 68, 69, 71, 76, 77, 79, 80–4, 86–9, 91, 92, 100–3, 105, 113
McPherson, James B., 21, 30, 53, 54, 61, 62, 76, 77, 79, 80, 82–4, 86–8, 90, 93, 94, 100–2, 113
Memphis, 19, 20, 29, 34, 37, 40, 41, 43, 48, 49, 50, 51, 53, 57, 69, 71, 72, 74, 84, 99, 105, 113, 122, 127
Mississippi river, geography

and strategic position, 8–11, 34
Mississippi, State of, 14–8
Montgomery, James E., 27, 40, 41
naval attack on Vicksburg, 41–3
Navy, United States, 34
New Madrid, 26, 34, 35, 37, 54
New Orleans, 9, 10, 11, 16, 24, 25, 28, 34, 37–40, 44, 45, 68, 75, 94, 123, 127
Ord, Edward O. C., 21, 29, 113, 117
orders of battle, 29–32
passage of the Mississippi at Bruinsburg, 79
Pemberton, John C., 22–4, 32, 47, 50, 52, 69, 74–6, 78–81, 83–4, 96, 97, 99, 100, 103–5, 107, 108, 112, 115–21, 123, 124
Porter, David D., 24–6, 38, 41–4, 47, 48, 50–2, 56–8, 61–71, 77–9, 81, 82, 94, 99, 105–7, 114–16, 119, 120, 122, 125
Port Hudson, 65–8
Queen of the West, 41, 43, 44, 45, 49, 56, 57, 58, 65, 67, 68
relief of Vicksburg, Confederate attempts at, 107–8, 113–14, 116–17
Scott, Winfield, 16
Sherman, William Tecumseh, 20, 30, 47–53, 62–4, 68, 69, 71, 79–83, 85, 87, 88, 91, 93, 94, 99, 100–4, 106–8, 113, 114, 122, 125, 126
siegeworks before Vicksburg, Union, 104–5, 111–12
strategy, Union, 34–7, 41, 46–7, 53–4; see also Grant
surrender of Vicksburg, 117–20
uniforms, 33
Van Dorn, 41, 48, 52, 83
Vicksburg, geography and strategic position, 11*ff*
Walnut Hills, see Chickasaw Bluffs
warship types, 36–8
weapons, 33
Wilson, James Harrison, 60–1
Yazoo river and pass, 8, 11, 12, 28, 43, 44, 48–52, 55, 56, 58–63, 65, 67, 68, 79, 80, 94, 97, 99, 100, 105, 111, 122, 126